Are We Being Honest to God?

Brian Pointer

Typeset in Sabon Lt Std

Design, typesetting and publishing by UK Book Publishing

www.ukbookpublishing.com

ISBN: 978-1-912183-52-4

Are We Being Honest to God?

"Vision to see, faith to believe, courage to do."
(Union Street Station, Los Angeles, USA.)

Introduction

When the Anglican bishop John T. Robinson published his controversial book "Honest to God" in 1963, there was a huge outcry from within the establishments and conservative elements of various Christian Churches, including the Catholic Church. Apart from the many radical ideas about God and the Christian Churches in the book, he is also remembered for his focus on "God" not being "out there" but being "the ground of our being", totally involved in our nature and life. The writing of his book was the result of a long period of gradual realisation that he wasn't being really 'honest' to himself and therefore to God in his Christian and ecclesial life. He came to realise, if he was really honest, that the "religious frame" in which the Christian faith had become enclosed, needed to be radically questioned if that Faith was to be defended. (p.9)

Fifty years later, after I had been re-examining my own views on the Catholic Church for some time, I read his book once again with a much greater degree of attention. I have often found that re-reading a book after having gone through many years of different experiences in life, it is like looking through fresh eyes. I see things which I had not been aware of the first time, or if I was aware of them they did not seem either relevant or important at that stage of my life. There is no doubt that I was drawn back to it, particularly to the significance of its title,

1

because of my own development of views about the "religious frame" of the Catholic Church, of which I have been a member for 58 years.

It is not easy to be really honest, to be really confident in expressing what we really believe for fear of being criticised and indeed condemned for our views. At the same time, there is that fear that perhaps we are in error in believing certain things and therefore we should not give them voice and lead people astray if we are in positions of leadership and influence. I have to admit that many times in the past I have refrained from speaking out and being really honest for fear of being wrong in what I believe. Of course there were many times when I was in fact wrong to believe certain things, but this is part of growing in understanding and knowledge throughout our lives, as long as we are prepared to move on in our belief and understanding.[1] However, there comes a time when it is right to be really honest and to air our views which have been tempered in the cauldron of life, hewn and moulded through experience, nourished by the wisdom of others, and, in the case of the Church, strengthened by that mysterious 'sense of the faith' (Lt.sensus fidei) which is a kind of instinct for what is really at the heart and root of the Christian faith.

Being honest about our beliefs and doubts is also about being 'honest to God' and this can be problematical if our own image of God is a distorted one because of the way God has been presented to us throughout our lives. Much of our belief and understanding about God and the Church is influenced by either our parents or friends and local priests and on a wider scale by bishops, Popes and theologians. Our *personal* faith in the person and teachings of Jesus Christ, the Son of God, has been formed and coloured by those external experiences as well as internal spiritual insights. Unfortunately, mainly

---

1   See New Testament "Letter to the Hebrews" 6:1.

because of the way that relationship between the 'people' and those holding offices in the Church developed over many years, indeed over hundreds of years, our image of God developed through the lens of that relationship. If that relationship is built on the 'rock, the foundations of the Gospel, then our image of God is formed through the life and teachings of his Son. If that relationship has been built on the shifting 'sand' of an image of God invented in the minds of leaders and guides who value power and control more than the love and truth of the Gospel, then our own image of God can become distorted through our blind obedience to such authority. If we are not careful, not honest to God by keeping ourselves connected to the sources of our faith, the Gospel of Jesus Christ, we can easily substitute that vital relationship with the image of God revealed by Jesus with one that has been distorted through loss of vital parts of that connection.

This development in the Church of an authoritarian relationship between those chosen to be leaders and guides and 'the people of God' is, as I suggest in the chapter on 'authority', one of the main reasons for the existence of a distorted image of God expressed in power and control rather than guiding and leading. The essential principle of the relationship between followers of Jesus as one of faith, hope and love, embodied in the biblical Greek concept of 'koinonia' i.e. fellowship and communion, became subjected to the power embodied in an 'authority' not only in teaching but also in controlling what the members of the Church could think and actually do. This power over the thoughts, actions and faith of Catholics developed to such an extent that there grew the phenomenon of what one theologian has described as "the unconditional passiveness" of large sections of the People of God.[2]

---

2   Karl Lehmann "Readings in Church Authority" p.190.

What has this got to do with being honest to God? This passivity of the people, and I include myself being in this state at different times of my Catholic life, is one of the results of the oppressive nature of our relationship with 'authority' as expressed in power and control rather than guiding and leading. It has got to the point now where most Catholics who do no more than attend Mass on a Sunday do not know that they are oppressed.[3] To suggest that their life and practice of Christian faith is so tightly controlled that they cannot express true honesty of belief and doubt is to invite a defensive response of denial or simply one of resignation to the status quo.

To say that myself or anyone has the correct understanding of the Christian faith and its implications for this world, is an example of arrogance of which we are all too familiar with inside and outside the Church. However, to be honest about what we believe is an act of true humility, for we are baring our heart and soul to God and others, even though we are afraid of what we say being shot down in flames! It is not about telling others what they should believe but being honest about what I believe after many years of going through various experiences, of many changes of thought, of battling emotions, of familiarity with the Bible, of studying deep theological and philosophical tomes as well as the simpler yet more enlightening and prophetic writings and sayings.

When I now look back over those years, often I have asked myself the following question: what has been the primary motivation for my adherence to the Christian faith and my membership of the universal (catholic) Christian Church? Was it originally a sense of duty to my parents who made sure that my sister, brothers and myself were brought up with some experience and knowledge of Christianity which led to my own free commitment? Perhaps it was that 'gift of faith' from God

---

3   Paul Lakeland, "The Liberation of the laity" p.187.

that the priests and bishops often taught us is the impetus which motivates us to become disciples of his Son, Jesus Christ. I am sure that both of these were part of my development of 'being a Christian', but to be really honest, without an awareness of the 'evidence', that is the truths of the Gospel, which justify and convince me in my faith and commitment, I would not have continued. Over the years I have come to realise that faith is not blind but is dependent on evidence upon which it is based. The author of the New Testament "Letter to the Hebrews" defines such faith as: *"the essence of things hoped for, the evidence of things not seen."* (11:1) (my translation). Faith requires "solid food" (5:12), that is, based on the truths of the Gospel of Jesus Christ which give us the reason for the hope that is within us.[4]

Heart and Mind

In my search for justification for the doctrines and practices of the Catholic Church, nevertheless I am conscious of the role of the 'heart' in that endeavour, whatever that may signify in human nature. There is no doubt that the interaction of our human faculties is still largely a mysterious fact of life. Scientists are now at the stage where they can tell us and even show us how the brain works, for example in relation to neural responses to emotions such as fear and excitement. However, finding similar empirical evidence of such notions as 'mind' and 'will' is not yet possible. The notion of us having 'heart' other than the physical pump in our bodies is not something subject to empirical proof. It has for a long time been associated with the human spirit, which drives or motivates us to will or not will a particular response or action. Various sayings have arisen such as being hard-hearted, soft-hearted, tender-hearted, cold-

---

hearted, light-hearted, broken-hearted. At difficult times we are said to reach down to the bottom of our hearts.

A few years ago I came across an old book of limericks, some funny, some serious, some mysterious. The value of limericks are their brevity which impels the writer to enclose the essential theme in just a few lines yet attract our attention by their musical rhyming rhythm. When I was writing a parish catechetical tract on the subject of 'heart and mind' I composed a limerick to express the important union of heart and mind in matters of faith. I was trying to counter the dichotomy of the two, very often found at parish level, where you would hear that faith is from the 'heart' and not of the mind:

There was a young man who said
That 'heart' was better than 'head',
But when his heart searched for God
It was his head which gave the nod
And his spirit was nourished by 'bread'.

Any teaching needs to be convincing for me to accept it, to own it in heart and mind, for it to become part of my belief and faith. I was trying to show that our relationship with God can only really be experienced and expressed in our fully integrated human nature through faith *and* reason, through heart (spirit?) and mind. For me, this means that holistic approach is important, not for the original impetus that may well be enclosed in the mists of my early life, but for my subsequent motivation and growth. When I listen to or read the teachings of our official Church leaders and guides or to theologians, I ask myself the question: on what foundation, on what evidence found in the teachings and life of Jesus and his first apostles is this particular teaching or practice based? In other words, on what is this teaching justified? How does it stand up in relation to the Gospel message? Is it merely the fact that it is taught by a particular person who perhaps has high office in the Church and therefore in a spirit of obedience I accept it as true? Is that 'unconditional passiveness' really faith in Jesus Christ, or does it prove to be neither faith nor belief when it is faced with the realisation that some of these teachings and practices have very little or no connection with the Gospel? The history of the Church is littered with such instances of errors in teaching and practice by those leaders and guides who consciously or unconsciously lost that vital communion with the Gospel. The testing standard is not the status quo of the Church, but the Gospel of Jesus Christ.[5] This theme runs through all the following three chapters on worship, priesthood and authority.

This does not mean that all of us have to achieve a very detailed knowledge of all of the truths of our faith, but it does mean that we have a *right* and a *duty* to constantly seek more understanding of those truths which give the reason for the hope that is in us. Pope John Paul II, although he did not move forward the reforms needed in the forms and structures of the Church, nevertheless made the very important point about one of the consequences of a lack of motivation to learn more about our faith, *"With a false modesty, people rest content with partial and provisional truths, no longer seeking to ask radical questions about the meaning and ultimate foundation of human, personal and social existence."*[6] It is interesting to note the use of the word 'radical' which comes from the Latin word 'radix' meaning 'root'. I am not sure that he was particularly amenable to those who posed radical questions about the official teachings and practices of the Church! However, in the context of 'faith seeking understanding' he was right about the danger of being content with half-truths. He probably would not have agreed with me in saying that perhaps we are content

---

5   Hans Kung "Structures of the Church" 1964, p.84.
6   Encyclical "Faith and Reason" ("Fides et Ratio") 1998. Para.11.

to stay where we are in our understanding because of the way the truths of our faith are given to us within the Church as requiring only our obedient acceptance rather than our assent of mind and heart. Whatever and wherever the reality of the 'heart' is, it can only be part of our holistic and integrated humanity and as such can only be active in our expression of faith through the consciousness of our minds. This is why faith cannot be expressed and lived-out through the heart only or through the mind only. John Paul II put this point very clearly in his letter: *"Faith and reason, each without the other is impoverished and enfeebled. Deprived of what Revelation offers, reason has taken side-tracks which expose it to the danger of losing sight of its final goal. Deprived of reason, faith has stressed feeling and experience, and so runs the risk of no longer being a universal proposition.....and withering into myth or superstition."*[7]

Maybe the lack of emphasis on seeking that understanding of the truths of our faith that never loses connection with the Gospel of Jesus Christ has led us to accept that faith is 'caught rather than taught'. This particular slogan, which seems to have acquired the character of an unchallengeable truth in preaching and catechesis, has done significant harm to the movement towards an integrated approach to a more mature faith. As a half-truth this slogan has given strength to the idea that we do not have to really exercise our minds in matters of faith. This was surely not the intention of whoever originally composed that slogan, but without the other half of the truth it has caused many to think that they can rest content with their initial baptismal faith, as my experience of the widespread existence of that 'unconditional passiveness' proves the case. It equates to another old saying that 'faith is a gift', the full truth of which escapes us if it simply remains a slogan. Faith is indeed

---

7   "Faith and Reason" para.48.

a gift from God as is everything which God has revealed to us by his self-communication in his Son. But it is a gift which needs to be embraced with our whole being throughout our life or we run the risk of losing it. The New Testament "Letter to the Hebrews" puts great emphasis on this risk of us becoming "those that have fallen away" (Gk. parapesontas)[8] through lack of growth in our understanding: *"We ought then to turn our minds more attentively to what we have heard so that we do not fall away."*[9] Faith needs to be an 'informed faith' otherwise its roots will not receive the nourishment it needs to survive. Those roots, planted by the Gospel and given strength by the presence of the Holy Spirit, are offered nourishment through the word of God for us as 'partakers' of the life of his Son, the "bread of life". (John ch.6.)

Forms and structures

As well as the theology behind the teachings and practices of the Catholic Church, my concerns about this connection with the Gospel have also been about the forms and structures of the framework within which that theology is expressed and enclosed. These forms and structures have effects, good or bad, on the mission of the Church. They can either attract or repel, or simply reduce people to indifference through their experience of those forms and structures. Throughout all three subjects of worship, priesthood and authority, people's experience of how these are taught, presented and expressed, of the forms and structures within which they are obliged to live-out their faith, is vital to their continuing allegiance to the institution in which its leaders exercise control.

---

8   Hebrews 6:6.
9   Ibid. 2:1.

I have no problem with having forms and structures to enable us to have the ability, opportunity, indeed the right and duty, to express our faith, not only in communal settings but also in carrying out our discipleship in the mission of the Church. Where I do have strong objection is to that idea which is prevalent in the minds of those who place undue value in preserving previous forms and structures which, even if they had some benefit in the past, are no longer serving the Gospel in the present age. Form is there to express that which, at the same time, enables its purpose. If the form is designed merely to preserve the status quo and to enable office-holders to exercise control enforced by a set of laws (e.g. Canon Law), its form then becomes a 'stumbling block' to what should be its purpose.

Charles Davis put this danger in very forcible terms when he wrote in 1967: *"To the extent that a Christian body betrays its mission to save its institutional position or existence, it ceases to be the Church of Christ. It has lost its Christian raison d'etre."*[10] For a theologian of his standing at the time to claim that the actual institutional structures of the Catholic Church were getting in the way of Christ's mission in the Church was a much needed shock for those 'in charge' of the institution. However, as has been the way such critique is dealt with, Davis as a person and priest-theologian was attacked rather than the validity of his views appraised in a spirit of humility. What is clear to me now is that much of what he said and wrote is still justified today despite the attempts by individual and reform movements over the last fifty years to elicit change in that mindset of church office-holders.

Of course, there have been changes made for the good of the Church, and at the present time Pope Francis is doing his best to continue John XXIII's call to "update" ("aggiornamento") and

---

10   "A Question of Conscience" 1967. P.105.

return to the sources of the Christian faith ("resourcement")[11] in an effort to strip away those things which he sees as directly opposing Christ's mission or are unhelpful. However, as I am suggesting in the following chapters, the problem is much deeper than the changes needed in the forms and structures which enclose worship, priesthood and authority. I maintain there are underlying fault-lines in the theological justification supporting their very existence. Whatever changes are made, and some of them are clearly necessary, without a reappraisal of their connection, their life-giving relationship, with the whole of the Gospel of Jesus Christ, the Church's worship, priesthood and authority will not be 'honest to God' because their image of God will not be that revealed by his Son.

Honest to myself?

When I first experienced the motivation to write this book, it was the realisation that all through my life, despite my commitment to the Catholic Church and deep involvement in parish and diocesan work, there were these nagging thoughts often coming to the surface that in certain areas of Church teaching and practice I was not really being honest to God about my doubts as to their validity in the light of the Gospel. When I look at the opportunities I was given to embrace those teachings and practices, to come to know more about God's self-communication in and through Jesus his Son, to grow in a personal relationship with not only the very idea of 'God' but also with the reality of his presence through their Spirit, I am somewhat surprised as to where I am now! Perhaps this is the effect of the "God of surprises".[12]

---

11   Address to the Council of Vatican II "Gaudet Mater Ecclesia" 1962.
12   Gerard W.Hughes "God of Surprises" 1985.

11

It may be helpful to any reader to see where I am coming from in setting out my thoughts in the following chapters on worship, priesthood and authority, the three main problem areas of Church life. These thoughts are not the product of recent experience but are the present position of a long journey of different experiences, some good, some bad, some indifferent, but always without losing my belief in the existence of God and faith in the person and teachings of Jesus Christ. Often I ask myself the question: what were those influences and experiences which have led my journey of faith to where I am now?

I was introduced to the Christian faith at a very early age when my parents sent their three sons to the local Sunday School and the later Bible School attached to the Congregational church. When I look back to that experience, it was mainly a good one. Maybe this was due to the simplicity of the presentation being about right for a boy growing up between the ages of 7 and 16 yrs at a time in the 1940s and 50s when everyday life was less complicated than it is now, especially for teenagers.

I must have had some idea of this 'God' as being a real person even though a very mysterious one whom I could not see but I could speak to in prayer. One significant moment very often springs to mind when I think about that time when I was about 9 or 10 years old. A visiting minister was speaking to us about the effect on this 'God' when we do not behave well. He said that God was very sad and disappointed when this happened. I remember this having a significant effect on me at the time. It was the realisation that this mysterious God was, first of all, aware of whom I was and concerned about what I did! Putting aside the later thoughts about whether God possesses the human characteristics of sadness and disappointment, that realisation marked the beginning of my Christian faith.

It was not until I was eighteen that I came into personal contact with Catholics through a friend at work who invited me to stay with his family in Ireland. It was there that I was faced with a different Christian culture in which there was total adherence to the teachings and rules of the Roman Catholic Church. The local priests were the focus of not only those teachings and practices but were a major influence in the moral and civic life of the towns. However, what really influenced me in becoming a 'Catholic' was the realisation that the Church could trace its 'apostolic authority' right back to Christ's first apostles, particularly that of the office of the Pope being the successor of St.Peter. When I look back now, the fact that I had a grounding in the Bible during my teenage years, that unbreakable link of the Catholic Church with the first apostles and authors of the Bible became important to me.

After becoming a Catholic I immersed myself in the life of a parish in West London where I met many new friends. That friendship was very important to me as I was the only Catholic in my family, who were not exactly against the idea but neither were they for it. It was during the next couple of years that the idea of becoming a Catholic priest started forming in my mind. It is difficult to identify the reasons for this desire but the example of those priests I met was clearly a major factor. Perhaps the motivation was a 'calling' from God, as it was described at that time? Only God knows.

Having approached my parish priest and asked the question as to whether becoming a priest was possible for me, it became clear that I would need a proficiency in Latin. Having left Grammar school at fifteen in order to earn money at some kind of work, I followed my love for woodwork and became a carpenter. Money was always very tight at home, mainly because my dad was very often ill, so our contributions were very important. Latin had not been on the agenda! At that time, believe it or not, a candidate for the priesthood of my age of twenty one was classed as a 'late vocation', so I entered a college for late vocations at Campion House, Osterley in order to learn Latin with further education in English language and literature, Church history and the 'spiritual life'. In many ways those residential two years of experiencing a hot-house of learning and experiencing Catholicism under Jesuit teachers was of immense value.

It was at Osterley that I made a decision to become a priest in the 'missions' and not in one of the English dioceses. I was accepted by the bishop of British Guiana and I was to continue my training first at Allen Hall, St. Edmund's, Ware, and then at a seminary in Trinidad. It is striking when I look at the contrast between the numbers of candidates for the priesthood at Allen Hall then (1963) as around 100 over the six-year training period, and the present day where often there are less than ten, and in some seminaries only one or two reaching ordination.

During that first year of philosophy at Allen Hall you became totally immersed in what it would mean to be a priest, in thought, word and deed, as well as all the trappings of dress and liturgical functions. It was a good time for me and an exciting one with Pope John XXIII trying to throw open the doors of the Church for some fresh air by calling the Second Vatican Council. We were fortunate to have among the staff of priests, Hubert (Bert) Richards the respected Scripture scholar, and Charles Davis the leading English theologian, and Peter de Rosa as our philosophy professor, all of whom had the foresight and courage to try and move-on the Church's understanding of itself, at great cost to themselves.

During this time I never once doubted that the existence of an ordained priesthood was justified for the mission of the Church, but doubts about my suitability for the compulsory celibate life of the priest began to surface. Eventually, after much soul-searching, I left Allen Hall and returned to my life at home. Those three years were of immense value to me in many different ways, particularly for the knowledge and experience of the Catholic Church I had gained in such a short time, but also the influence of friends and teachers who enabled me to open my mind and heart to the truths of the Gospel.

Throughout my life as a very fortunate husband and father over the following thirty years or so, Catholic life in its faith and practice was very much at the centre of my life. This was also true in my work as a police officer where the extremes in society would often challenge my pre-conceived ideas about human nature and issues of justice and social philosophy. Throughout my career, from beat officer to Inspector, from uniform patrol to several years as a detective, that time I had spent on studying for the priesthood continued to be a significant influence on my religious life. However, as time went on, like many other Catholics, questions in my mind about the teachings, practices and laws of the Church became more insistent for answers.

After 25 years, I retired from the Force in order to take up a five-year theology degree course through the Maryvale Institute at Birmingham with the Pontifical University, Maynooth. At the time, Maryvale was the only Vatican approved Catholic institution in England offering such distance-learning courses. I wanted to be able to answer those recurring questions about the theology behind the doctrines and practices of the Church. The course was rigorous and I had to be very disciplined in my daily study, but it was well worth the effort and cost in the degree of understanding Catholicism such a course provides. I went on to complete the Master's degree in Catholic theology in order to explore certain areas more deeply, particularly the relationship of human freedom with the official teaching on God's 'grace' in his gift of the Holy Spirit.

At the same time as this search for answers, my subsequent work at parish and diocesan level in ecumenism and catechesis has also been important in this journey of faith. Being involved in the annual RCIA[13] groups, parish councils, ecumenical activities, diocesan catechesis, and many liturgical activities,

---

13 "Rite for the Christian Initiation of Adults", consisting of weekly sessions for those contemplating becoming members of the Catholic Church.

has made me more aware of the many good disciples of Christ at work in the Catholic Church, despite the existence of unconvincing theology underpinning some prominent institutions and practices. This knowledge has also made me aware of those many Catholics throughout the UK and the world who, courageously and prophetically, are trying to draw attention to those teachings, practices and structures which are not underpinned by the principles of the Gospel, by forming movements for reform and renewal in response to the beginnings at Vatican II.[14]

The bare bones of the above summary of my journey of faith is not meant to be an autobiographical story but a helpful attempt, I hope, for any reader to see where I am coming from for my present position on the Church. This is not an attempt to write academic essays, as is plain for academics to see, but rather to try to express my thoughts in reasonably plain language, using my experience and academic studies in order to give solid reasons for my opinions. It is inevitable perhaps that, sometimes, I have had to use terminology which is not part of everyday discourse but is that which is used by office-holders and pastors of the Church. My purpose in writing this book is to take part in the debate on the Church, which in order to fulfil its mission from Christ must always be ready to accept renewal and reform. As an introduction to the three chapters on worship, priesthood and authority, I have tried to show that the views expressed in those chapters did not just come out of 'thin air', as though they have no roots. Yes, they are radical views, but only in the true sense of that term of being 'of the roots', together with being truly honest to myself and more importantly 'honest to God'.

---

14   E.g. "A Call to Action" in UK. (www.acalltoaction.org.uk); "We Are Church" (International); "American Catholic Council" (USA).

Christian Worship

The one activity of Catholics which for most is their only formal action as members of the Catholic Church is their attendance at 'Mass' or 'celebration of the Eucharist'. What is their experience of this activity? What is more to the point, what is my experience? It would be foolish to try and explain what others think about such experience, for that would be presumptive without a very thorough survey even though anecdotal evidence suggests that there are many negative reactions. I can only express my own reaction, not only in the present but also the development of experience over the 58 years of being a Catholic.

When I became a Catholic at the age of eighteen it was the beginning of the experience of being part of a world-wide organised religious institution, one that could trace its historical roots back to the first Apostles. At the time, this awareness of its 'authenticity' was the one thing which motivated me to find out more about this Church. From then on I attended Mass every Sunday and on other occasions during the week and became a 'committed' Catholic.

This obligation of 'attending Mass', of being present at what the priest was doing at the altar, was very much the way that most of us came to regard 'going to Church' as the norm. We were there to witness the priest acting on our behalf in his role of offering 'the sacrifice of the Mass' for us and for certain named persons. At that time, our actions mainly consisted in answering 'amen' to certain prayers and more importantly to receiving 'Holy Communion' by taking and eating the wafers of bread (the wine later) which, through the actions and words of the priest, had been changed into the body of Christ by the Holy Spirit. Much of the prayers and actions by the priest at this time (1960s) were conducted by the priest in an almost private way with his back to the people and very often with his words inaudible.

Much has changed since then, especially after the Council of Vatican II, with the congregation much more involved and the words and actions of the priest more accessible. However, the structure and the essential theology of the Mass has remained much the same today, yet the circumstances, culture and education of the people attending has dramatically changed. At the same time, in the West, less and less people are attending Mass, despite priests still telling them that it is a 'mortal sin' to deliberately miss it. Of course, there are areas in the world where attendance at Mass is still good and even growing, but one of the reasons for this can be found in historical and cultural factors, e.g. in African countries.

The initial question is whether the decline in attendance is a loss of personal faith in Jesus Christ or a loss of faith in the *institution* of the Church? What was the experience of being at Mass for those who no longer attend? Perhaps it was not the Mass itself which turned them away but a loss of respect for the 'authority' of those church office-holders whose role is to 'preach the Gospel', but also who preach conformity to the rules and regulations of the institution.

In the meantime, apart from my own accrued knowledge of many of the comments made by Catholics over many years, I look at my own experience of taking part in the liturgy of the Mass. When I look back I can see that even when I was a passive attender, accepting that what was being said and done was part of being a Catholic, there were questions in my mind about whether this was really what Christian worship was all about. Like many others, I suspect, I would dismiss these thoughts and rely on the idea that the 'Church', i.e. the hierarchy, knows best.

Christian or pagan?

The idea that the forms of this 'worship' seem to be more pagan than Christian would not go away. What do I mean by this? When recently I re-read John Robinson's book "Honest to God", the point he made about re-thinking our concept of God seemed to me to be at the very core of any serious thinking about worship. What we think and believe about God clearly determines what we think about worship. On the other hand, how we worship shows what we think God is like. Is our image of God formed by language and practices of worship which contain elements of pagan ideas? Where and to whom do we go to find out what God is like in order to relate to him/her? For is this not what worship is really all about, a relational response to God who is always in a relationship with us? A union so fundamental that like husband and wife, loved and lover, it is never possible for us not to be related to God, even though we often do not show this in our lives. If 'grace' is God's loving action mediated by the Son through the Holy Spirit, it is the form of God's relatedness.[15] He is not 'out there, at such a distance from us that we have to adopt forms of worship which express a relationship based on subservience and obeisance, but rather his self-communication in the person of his Son expressing that closeness which is nearer to us than we are to ourselves.

---

15   Gunton, Colin.E. "Intellect and Action: Elucidations on Christian Theology and the Life of Faith." (2000) p.182.

"To whom should we go, Lord, for you have the words of eternal life."

This statement in John's Gospel (6:68) has always been for me one of the fundamental principles of the Christian faith. Together with the belief that Jesus was and is the 'Son of God', Peter's declaration of faith gives me the direction that my prayer life and worship should take. If I did not believe that Jesus, in himself and his words, shows us what God is like, I would have no motivation in seeking a relationship with an unknowable God. God's self-communication in the person and words of his Son is what makes that relationship possible. I now know something meaningful about God.

The next question follows: what exactly is it that Jesus the Son tells me about God his father? It is the answer to this question which should tell me something about the way and the manner I should relate to God, both in my private life and in any communal gathering of believers expressed as 'church'. If the nature and manner of my reciprocal communication to God's approach, privately and communally, as expressed in what became known as 'worship', does not relate to what God reveals about himself in and through his Son, then it is based on an unreal person. My image of God is unreal and therefore my acts of worship are inappropriate and fruitless. This is what John Robinson was getting at when he wrote the following:

"What looks like being required of us, reluctant as we may be for the effort involved, is a radical new mould, or metamorphosis, of Christian belief and practice. Such a recasting will, I am convinced, leave the fundamental truth of the Gospel unaffected. But it means that we have to be prepared for everything to go into the melting, even our most

cherished religious categories and moral absolutes. And the first thing we must be ready to let go is our image of God himself."[16]

If my image of God is unreal, that is, it is not conformed to that shown in Jesus the Son, then my worship becomes idolatry. Clearly, my knowledge of God can only be incomplete, for I will only be able to see him 'face to face' once I have passed through death to that new promised life. If this is true then in order to answer the above question I need to identify those aspects of the image which Jesus did reveal and how these affect the way(s) I respond.

The most important image for me is that of Jesus himself as Son, *"I and the Father are one." (John 10:30); If you know me, you will know my Father also. From now on you do know him and have seen him."* (John 14:7). Apart from these two examples, there are many other references in the New Testament in which we are familiar with this teaching of Jesus being the reflection or "radiance" of the Father.[17] The image above all which is displayed by Jesus is that of a person who is full of love and truth, whose mission is to bring that love and truth to all. Everything else depends on this fundamental teaching; the truth about ourselves, creation, God the Father, Son and Holy Spirit, and their love for mankind.

How do we respond to this loving approach in our private and communal life? Do we engage in some kind of worship as our response, once we declare belief and faith in Jesus? If so, does the form and content of this worship conform to that image of God revealed by Jesus? Does our understanding of the concept of worship distort that image?

---

16   "Honest to God" p.124
17   E.g. Letter to the Hebrews.1:3.

The practice of 'worship'

Most Catholic Christians adopt practices of worship which they become aware of as part of being members of the institution of the Catholic Church from an early age. Even those who became members later in life, such as myself at 18, automatically accept the concept of 'worshipping' God and enter into those practices, such as 'the celebration of the Mass' and many other rituals and use of symbols. Increasingly, over the years I have experienced unease over the whole concept of worship as practised in many aspects of church life. In trying to work out what it is that causes me to question the forms and manner of these practices, I began to realise that it was to do with their relationship to the image I had formed of Jesus, and therefore my image of God the Father.

A relationship of love

This image of Jesus has been formed throughout my life by reading the New Testament, the writings of the early fathers of the Church and many other Christians throughout the two millenniums of Christianity, as well as listening to many talks and homilies. Not only absorbing their ideas but also applying my own mind in seeking understanding of the person and teachings of Jesus. What is it about him that makes me shy away from many of the ideas and practices of Christian worship? It is not easy to crystalize my thoughts into one concept but the one thing that stands out is his desire to express the love of his Father to all he met while on earth. This was not done in the way that many of his listeners were used to experiencing the relationship of master and servant, of king and subject, of conqueror and conquered, nor was it done in the way that many of them and their ancestors had seen other peoples' relationships with their pagan gods, and unfortunately had incorporated some of their ideas and practices in their own rituals of worship.

Jesus showed that his Father wanted a relationship with everyone that is of *the loved and lover*. How do we relate to one another when there is true love between us? In what manner do we communicate with each other? How do we address each other? If Jesus has shown that our relationship with God his Father is one that is based on love then where does the concept and practice of worship fit in this relationship? In this context of *personal* worship I am not considering every aspect of the multi-faceted content of the 'liturgy' of the Church in which we take part in what is called the 'efficacious signs' of the sacraments and other devotional practices. However, how we regard our personal relationship with God is of great significance to that content and the forms which it takes. If our image of God is not that which conforms to what Jesus his Son has revealed, then whatever else we do in the practices of the liturgy of the Church will not be 'honest to God'. It is then that the image of God in the practices of communal worship can become distorted. What kind of distortions am I talking about?

Approaching God

One of the trends which have grown throughout the history of the Church is the habit of approaching God, whether privately or communally, in an idolatrous, pagan form of subservience. I say 'idolatrous' because this approach is to a god who is unreal, not God the Father revealed by Jesus. I say 'pagan' because this image relates to that God invented by human minds. This is the result of using language and concepts which are alien to our time and culture but which those in office regard as necessary to preserve the 'tradition' of the Church. However, it does the exact opposite by forming a distorted image of God through constant use of misappropriate language and concepts. The language of many prayers, both official and private, and the manner in which they are said, have an idolatrous and ingratiating character. There is a consistent effort to please God in such a way that it is reminiscent of the images of the Roman pagan practices of worship which seek to elicit good fortune from their gods.

The history of the Church's language of 'sacrifice' in the context of worship shows this tendency for an approach to God where there is the sense of trying to please and appease. How did this come about when it is compared to the example set by Jesus? Perhaps it all stems from the appropriation of ideas and practices from the Roman pagan rituals of worshipping their pagan gods during the subsequent centuries after Christianity became absorbed into Roman civic life. There is no doubt that this turn of events had a significant effect on the development of practices and ideas in Christian worship, particularly in relation to the doctrines of sacrifice and priesthood up to the present day. This led to our approach to God being formed out of an image of Him as an all-powerful God who can be appeased by our obedience to his will as revealed through a cultic priesthood in cultic rituals.

A few examples will illustrate this tendency to approach and address God in this manner. Many of the official prayers begin by addressing God as 'Lord God almighty', or 'Almighty God'. This particular form of address, if we were really honest with ourselves, evokes that concept of adulation and appeasement which is so redolent of the pagan relationships to their invented gods. It is a clear example of that approach which is so inappropriate to that image of God revealed by his Son. It sets the tone for that kind of approach which thinks that addressing God this way will put us in good standing with him by acknowledging his power. This may have been the way that the priests and prophets at one time sometimes addressed

God, but Jesus revealed that his Father desired a more personal approach which demonstrated that love between father and his children, between the loved and the lover. We only have to really listen to the words of Jesus in the fourth Gospel to see this basis of love for our approach to God: *"Anyone who loves me will keep my word, and my Father will love him and we shall come to him and make a home in him."* (John 14:21) The depth and closeness of such a personal love completely precludes any idea of a God who desires us to address him in an impersonal and ingratiating manner in order to honour him. As I shall later suggest, giving 'honour' to God has nothing to do with adulatory titles of address.

Talking to God

Throughout the liturgy of the Church there are numerous examples of inappropriate language which distorts the image of God as revealed by Jesus. Some of these are so familiar to us that we don't really think about what we are saying or meaning. One such example in the liturgy of the Mass is the congregation's response to the prayers of the priest during the 'preparation of the gifts', *"Blessed be God for ever"*. Whether we place the emphasis on the whole word 'blessed' or both syllables as in 'bless-ed', are we simply addressing God as the priest has just done or are we addressing nobody in particular, just making a statement? Whatever each individual thinks it means, it is not only inappropriate language for our time but is also a result of that distorted image of God which results in uttering meaningless praise. I could, with many other commentators, write many words about the derivation and different meanings of the term 'blessed', but that would miss the point that it simply becomes a mantra rather than saying something which reflects a true image of God.

Another example of where this idea that adulatory praise is something desired by God and therefore gives us a distorted image can be found in the Eucharistic Prayers. Again, we are so familiar with this 'acclamation' that we sing it without thinking whether it is appropriate for our image of God: *"Holy, Holy, Holy Lord God of hosts, heaven and earth are full of you glory. Hosanna in the highest."* This became a popular acclamation over many centuries, set to wonderful music in many different ways, but also recited without music in many churches. However, as an example of addressing God, it reinforces that conception of God as someone upon whom we should heap inappropriate praises of his power and might rather than addressing him as the loved to the lover. 'Praising' God has nothing to do with the language of adulation but is everything to do with honouring God in Creation by acknowledging all that he is doing out of love for us.

It also highlights that habit of those who write these prayers and hymns of using repetitive words, as though using one word will not be enough. This is even more pronounced in the many prayers where whole sentences are repeated over and over again in the same prayer. One example is the penitential prayer at the beginning of the Mass: *"through my fault, through my fault, through my most grievous fault"* as if God is not aware of what is in our hearts and minds when we say the first part! When I hear this I often think of what Jesus said in Matthew's Gospel, *"When you are praying, do not heap up empty phrases as the Gentiles do; for they think that they will be heard because of their many words. Do not be like them, for your Father knows what you need before you ask him."*(Matt.6:7). It also reminds me of the false humility of the character of Uriah Heep ("I'm humble, I am.") in Charles Dicken's perceptive novel 'David Copperfield'.

It was after this teaching that Jesus told us how to pray using the address *"Our Father"*. That prayer, which every Christian is familiar with, is a perfect example, first of all, of using the address which shows the kind of relationship God wants for us, and then using an economy of words to express the important content. It does not say everything that needs to be said but it is used by Jesus to show us the *way* we should pray. It is also significant that Jesus identifies those who use many words and empty phrases, for many of them worshipped gods other than the God of Israel. Here, the image of God as his Father causes us to use meaningful words and simplicity of language.

There are many examples of where the official prayers of the Church do in fact approach and address God simply as God the Father, but, paradoxically, there are also many instances where the form of address, and also the content, portrays a reluctance to move away from those historically conditioned forms of address which, although not intended to be, are based on a distorted image. Why is this so important an issue for me? My concern is that if we are led to view God in such contrast to what Jesus his Son has revealed, then our practices of worship are directed to an unreal God; we are not worshipping *"in spirit and truth"* (John 3:24)

Actions and body language in 'worship'

As well as the words we use we also show what we think about God in those actions which have become part of our practices of worship. I can remember when I first became a Catholic that the action of genuflecting before the 'Blessed Sacrament' as we entered the church building was one of the marks of being 'Catholic'. This, together with a kind of reverential awe throughout the Mass, especially at the moment of consecration of the bread and wine and their elevation, created that atmosphere that we were in a special presence of God.

Some say today that we have lost that reverential awe because the atmosphere is much more relaxed and noisier and people do not seem to show the same respect and reverence that was shown in those earlier times. There is no doubt that the actions and body language of some members tends to suggest that their commitment to following the conventions and rules of attending and taking part in the Mass has diminished. However, is this lack of reverence due to a diminishing of their commitment to what 'the Mass' is all about, or, perhaps, a consequence of a cultural shift in attitude to conventions, or is it the result, in some, of a change in their ideas of the image of God?

There is no doubt that in my own case a change has occurred in my ideas about rules and conventions at communal acts of worship such as the Mass. Of course, I would not dream of showing disrespect to other members of the congregation through my actions, but my earlier commitment to carrying out all the required actions and attitudes according to convention and tradition has been changed by this desire to be really honest to that image of God revealed by Jesus. When I enter a church building to celebrate the presence of the resurrected Jesus at the Eucharist, I am less formal in my attitude and body language which before tended to be the response to a perceived distance between me and God. Over the years, my image of God has changed my attitude when being in his particular presence at Mass to that of entering and staying in a friendly atmosphere, for that was how Jesus celebrated that Last Supper he had with his friends. It is also in line with Jesus' image of God as 'Father' to us all, wherever we are and whatever we are doing. The atmosphere in Mass should, therefore, be one which demonstrates the love of friends and family, where Jesus' presence through his and the Father's Spirit brings not only us but also the stranger into that circle of love.

A circle of love and fellowship

However, the question arises as to whether the form and practices of the Mass, the celebration of the Eucharist, show and foster such a friendly and loving experience which is described in the original biblical Greek as 'koinonia' and translated as fellowship or communion? My experience is one of wide variation, from feeling part of such an expression of family fellowship to the experience of being an onlooker or outsider to what the priest was doing at an altar. This variation of experience appears to be common throughout the British Isles, and may well be the result of a distorted image of God which has led to a particular form of the celebration of the Last Supper whereby the emphasis was placed on priestly mediation rather than the communion ('koinonia') of that event.

That emphasis led to the ordained priest becoming the centre of attention and activity at a sacramental act of remembrance or commemoration initiated by Jesus' actions and words at that Last Supper. Of course, any communal gathering which has a particular focus needs some kind of direction to lead them through the particular actions and words applicable to its purpose. This is the function and role of the leader or presider, but he/she must never become so visible, so central of attention, that the congregation's presence and action becomes *mediated* through a single person. This brought me to consider the whole question of 'priesthood' and its corollary of 'mediation' which I will be dealing with in the next chapter because of its importance and relevance to our image of God.

Experiencing worship in 'the Mass'

In continuing the chain of thought about how our actions and body language express our understanding of the image of

God in our individual and communal activities, my search for honesty of belief led me to consider this experience of 'going to Mass'. What was I actually seeing and hearing? Are my expectations fulfilled or do I simply accept that it is something that I ought to do and often not regard it as a good experience? We all know that despite the content of some particular action it is *how* it is done that leaves the greatest impression. This is particularly important for the central communal activity of Catholics in the celebration of the Eucharist in the Mass. If it is right for the priest to be so central and visible, (this will be considered in the next chapter), then his words, actions, appearance and body language will be of utmost importance. It was the same for me as a police officer, teacher and catechist and for any person in a position of influence or authority. In the activity of priests we are taught by traditional teaching that our very future beyond death is at stake, so *how* they have an impact on us has serious consequences, if that is true.

There have been numerous instances where, by their attitude and behaviour some priests have caused Catholics to stop going to Mass and eventually losing whatever faith they had in the first place. Of course, priests are only human and can have the usual human failings and we can have too high expectations of them. We have put the priest on a pedestal and then expect him to be superhuman! However, this is not the real problem underlying the relationship between the people and priests. What is at the root of how the priest carries out his role is this whole question of the legitimacy of such an ordained priesthood, its manifestation and practice in relation to the original intention of Jesus. What should be the role of the leader of today's commemoration of the Last Supper, one of offering priestly sacrifice or that of a pastoral leader of the community's own 'remembrance' in that special communion with Jesus Our Lord? (see chapter on 'priesthood).

The nature of 'worship'

It is one of the unfortunate consequences of a distorted image of God that the word and concept of worship has become primarily related to what Christians do when they come to together in some kind of 'liturgical act' which has been arranged, ordered and controlled by leaders and office-holders of the Church's administration. We have become so used to describing our 'acts of worship' in this context that we have become inured to the use of language and concepts which not only have drawn us away from the revealed image of God but also have given us a very limited idea of that worship which is desired by God our Father. It is also unfortunate that the same word and concept is used in some pagan and neo-pagan religions in the context of appeasement and obeisance.

Nowhere in the Scriptures is worship actually defined. It is as though it was such a familiar concept to the people of Israel and the Jews at the time of Jesus and the early Church that the writers felt they had no need to explain the word. The development of this term and concept moved through various words, meanings and references throughout the Old Testament period. At one time it literally meant the body language of 'bending from the waist' to express an inward attitude of homage and respect.[18] This was particularly true in oriental customs and in pagan homage to the gods, but also was used in the OT to express surrender to the living and true God or a reaction to some divine revelation. Different words used in the Hebrew scriptures and their subsequent Greek translation (known as the Septuagint and designated by LXX) give additional meanings from which our English word 'worship' was developed. Some had the meaning 'to serve' and this was picked up in the Greek LXX by a word relating to the service of

---

18   D.G.Peterson "Worship", New Dictionary of Biblical Theology, 2000.

God, 'leitourgein', from which we get our word 'liturgy'. This meaning of 'service to God' was also used to include the kind of service where keeping His commandments and 'walking in his ways' was expressed. Sacrifice and other rituals, much of which was copied from other nations, were there to express reverence and faithfulness to God in the context of this service to God. Any deviation from this faithfulness was condemned as idolatry.[19]

True worship

What did Jesus reveal about the true worship that God desires from us? Surprisingly, when I consider how often the word 'worship' has been used in the history of the Church, it is only in the Gospel of John that I find any statement of Jesus which refers to 'true' worship. In chapter 4 Jesus meets a Samaritan woman at a well and in the conversation which follows there is discussion as to the proper place to worship God. But Jesus tells her that the nature and place of worship is about to change in a fundamental way:

"Jesus said to her, "Woman, believe me, the hour is coming, and is now here, when the true worshippers will worship the Father in spirit and truth, for the Father seeks such as these to worship him. God is spirit, and those who worship him must worship in spirit and truth." (4:23-24)

The Greek word used here, which was later translated into English as 'worship', comes from the verb meaning 'to give homage or allegiance to someone'. It is unfortunate that the translators decided upon that English word which also was used to designate that kind of obeisance and adulation in neo-pagan contexts. The kind of homage which is closer to the meaning

---

19   Ibid. p.856-7.

intended by the writer of the fourth Gospel would be that which we know as that 'devotion' between the loved and the lover. This is not a criticism of those scholars of NT Greek but rather the unfortunate development of the English usage of a term which had become accepted as appropriate. This is particularly important for today's language and culture in which mere acceptance of a particular word because of its traditional usage is no longer regarded as of sole importance. A contemporary example of this can be seen in the controversy surrounding the present official English translation from a traditional Latin version of the prayers of the Catholic Mass. The lack of any kind of meaningful terminology and syntax in these prayers is indicative of the error of assuming that the Latin version has some kind of traditional sacral authority and therefore should be followed for all time. The language of Christian worship, as service to God, has to be such that it is able to express the faith, hope and love of the people of God of the present time. This is not simply a question of using a particular form of words but about developing concepts and terminology which accurately reflect our belief and faith to those around us: *"A Christianity that ceases to develop new confessional language ceases to confess its faith to the contemporary world."*[20]

In spirit and truth.

What does this mean to worship in *spirit and truth*? Clearly it is different to the old ideas of worship as homage and obeisance expressed in cultic rituals of adulation and sacrifices. In addition, true worship is no longer to be tied to a particular earthly place such as a particular mountain or in Jerusalem (4:21), or indeed to a church building. It is now a person, Jesus Christ himself

---

20 Dunn "Unity & Diversity in the New Testament" p.58.

who replaces them and is where the Father's 'glory', i.e. his divinity, is acknowledged and served; where Jesus is, so is God the Father. Whereas before, the people only had access to God through the priests and the Temple, we now have access to the Father in and through the person of Jesus his Son. He is the 'bridge' for that personal union. Any outward sign of this, in our actions, words and attitudes, must reflect this truth. The old Latin maxim 'Lex orandi, lex credendi', 'the law of prayer (is) the law of belief/faith' is very relevant here. What we believe forms and informs our personal communication with God which we call 'prayer'. Prayer without belief is simply directed to no-one in particular, which is meaningless. Therefore, truths about God, about Jesus, and about ourselves, are essential in forming a true expression of our devotion.

What does it mean to worship in *spirit*? The Greek word used for 'spirit' (pneuma) is used by NT writers to designate both the human spirit and the Spirit of God, depending on the context. Sometimes, biblical scholars and commentators say that it can be used to mean both at the same time – a double meaning. From the context of this text we can see that it is about *our* acts of devotion which are not to be mere outward shows but of an inner spiritual reality. From the context of the Gospel as a whole, the gift of God's Spirit nourishes and inspires us, leading us to all truth, as John writes later in his gospel (16:13). This means that our worship, our expression of service to God and each other, is to arise from that new relationship of God's Spirit with our own spirit, from which we learn to give *true* worship in the way we live our lives. If our worship is to be a service of devotion to God then that can only be reflected not only at a communal Eucharistic gathering but also in our service and devotion to others.

34

True worship in the liturgy?

The question which now has to be asked is whether our acts of worship, in the second millennium since that revelation, have faithfully followed that teaching? Although there are instances in the Christian liturgy which clearly follow Jesus' teachings about *true* worship, the general approach to God the Father through his son, Jesus, is still very much influenced by that image of God which requires adulation and obeisance as the way of giving him honour or glory. It is clear from Jesus' teachings that we honour God by the way we carry-out his will in loving our neighbour, not in directing flowery phrases of adulation to God himself. This is vitally important for the celebration of the Eucharist at Mass and other related rituals and devotions. The practices of adulation, adoration and neo-pagan actions and words directed to God the Father can only be in direct contrast to that 'true worship' which relates to the true image of God revealed by Jesus. That revelation does not show that God wants such a relationship, nor does it show that we need to honour him in this way. If we persist in portraying such an image of God to others we become like those members of the Pharisees whom Jesus criticised by quoting the prophet Isaiah: *"This people honours me with their lips, but their hearts are far from me; in vain do they worship me, teaching human precepts as doctrines."* (Isaiah 29:13, Matt. 15:8-9)

Worship as manipulating God?

Another example of where a distorted image of God has influenced our ideas of worship is the growth over a long time of using prayer as a means of bargaining with God. This has, particularly, been promoted by those office-holders who have persistently encouraged people in this practice of 'quid pro quo' in order to get some kind of favour from God. The practice of using gifts of prayers such as novenas as well as various rites and vows to persuade God and the 'saints' to intervene in some way has been common for centuries. In particular, the practice of offering Masses (often with an accompanying payment) for the purpose of obtaining heavenly benefits for deceased relatives, or for help of the 'intentions' of those named, is a prime example of this false understanding of not only our relationship with God but also of the nature and purpose of the Eucharistic service at Mass.

In a recent article, in the context of 'corruption', Norbert Reck asks the question *"Is God subornable?* [21] The term 'suborn' is not one which readily comes to our lips in everyday language and is mainly used in a legal sense of trying to persuade or bribe someone to do something which is a response to a gift. The author is asking whether God can be persuaded by our offerings to bestow some favour which we desire. His investigation into the context of the Bible found that it is directly associated with the practice of sacrifice, particularly in the Old Testament religion of the Babylonians, but was rejected by the word of God of Israel through the Psalmist (Psalm 50) as though God needed an exchange of goods. There were to be sacrifices in Israel, but not as attempts to manipulate God, but instead sacrifices of thanksgiving, a practical acknowledgement of what people owe to God.[22] God knows what they need and gives of his own free will.

Likewise, the teachings of Jesus clearly show that God the Father knows what we need, and what is more, is aware of what is in our hearts and minds. His work of love through his Son and Holy Spirit cannot be manipulated by offerings of set

---

21 Art."Is God Subornable?" in International Journal of Theology "Concilium" 2014/5.
22 Ibid. p.112.

prayers, rites or sacrifices, but is his act of free love to which we respond in a sacrifice of thanksgiving in service and devotion. Our concerns and desires can be expressed from our hearts in conversation with Him in prayer and he wants us to ask for his help, but always acknowledging that his loving care for us is always active in the context of what is good for us and the salvation of his people.(see Matthew 7:7-11) The notion that God is *persuaded* by a 'performance and reward' relationship with his people is symptomatic of that distorted image of God which has corrupted the practice of Christian worship.

A web of inappropriate words

The worship which is acceptable to God as devoted service is that which gives glory to him by carrying out his will in our lives.[23] By this we acknowledge him personally and to others as being the source of all the gracious gifts we need to live a life of faith, hope and love. In this way we are showing his glory, his divine reality, through being disciples of his Son who is 'the radiance' of God's glory. But what does this really mean for us today? How can we get beneath the use of language which appears to many as being archaic, of being inappropriate for our time and culture?

One of the things I learned as a police detective when investigating a complex crime was that, despite all the confusing detail, I needed to narrow it down to what was the essential crime and then follow the evidence. This was particularly important in the case of fraud and deception. I had to keep that focus in mind in order not to be led on a false trail. Similarly, in my theological and biblical studies, I found that through keeping the focus on the essential point of a particular

---

23   Cf.Letter of Paul to the Romans 12:1-2.

ARE WE BEING HONEST TO GOD?

teaching I was able to keep clear of being caught in a web of words of a particular culture and time, which although I had to understand, nevertheless could prevent me from getting near the truth if I didn't keep that focus.

In our acts of worship today we are still using words and expressions which are not only inappropriate to our times and culture but also prevent us from devoting ourselves to God in spirit and truth and therefore acknowledging the true image of God. Here are a few examples of such words and phrases (underlined) from the Eucharistic Prayers in the revised missal:

* "these holy and _unblemished sacrifices_ which we offer you firstly for your holy Catholic Church"
* "and all your saints; we ask that through their _merits_ and prayers in all things we may be defended by your protecting help."
* "Therefore, Lord, we pray; _graciously_ accept _this oblation of our service_"
* "and _command_ that we be delivered from _eternal damnation_ and _counted_ among the flock of _those you have chosen._"
* "he took this _precious chalice_ in his holy and _venerable_ hands"
* "we, your servants and your holy people, offer to your _glorious majesty_"
* "_Be pleased to look upon these offerings with a serene and kindly countenance_"
* "_to your altar on high in the sight of your divine majesty_"
* "Look, we pray, upon _the oblation of your Church._"
* "give _kind admittance_ to your kingdom"
* "countless hosts of angels, who serve you day and night, _and gazing upon the glory of your face,_ glorify you without ceasing."

* *"Through him <u>the Angels praise your majesty, Dominions adore and Powers tremble before you. Heaven and the Virtues of heaven and the blessed Seraphim worship together with exultation.</u>"*

These are just a few examples to illustrate the kind of language which millions of Catholics hear every Sunday and in many churches every day of the week. Do we really hear in the sense of taking notice and digesting the meanings or are they the "noisy gongs or clanging of cymbals" [24] from which we turn away our ears? My own experience shows that the latter has become the case as time has passed and I have grown weary of listening to such language which so badly distorts the image of God revealed by his Son. This is tradition for the sake of tradition, not the 'handing-on' of truths which need to be expressed in the language of the times in order for those truths to be grasped by every generation. It is then that we can worship in spirit and truth. In chapter 17 of John's Gospel, where Jesus prays to his Father before going to his death on the cross, we can read a clear example of how we should pray. A complete contrast to those examples above.

Consequences of this distorted image

If this has affected my own experience of attending and taking part in the official acts of worship, has it not also affected others? This is hard to be specific but in my conversations with others, together with the rise in various reform movements in the UK, Europe and USA, there is evidence of dissatisfaction with the control exercised by office-holders over the people's freedom to worship in spirit and truth. I put it like that because

---

24   1Corinthians 13:1

the root of the problem, apart from the distorted image of God, lies in the questions about control and authority in the Church. (These two subjects are dealt with in the later chapter on 'authority'.)

There is no doubt that one of the major reasons for the decline in Mass attendance in many areas of this country is first of all the negative experience by many of attending something which, let's be honest, has become less and less relevant to their Christian faith. Time and time again through conversations with young and old, the same comments are heard, *"but it is so boring!"*; *"Once the priest starts going into his prayers at the altar, I switch off!"*; *"I find the Old Testament readings and the language of the prayers at the altar are simply irrelevant to my life."*; *"I only go for communion."* There are many others but the common theme is one where much of what goes on and the language and concepts used are something to stoically bear because we have been conditioned to the concept of obligation to attend, under pain of sin (still officially 'mortal'!) if we don't without good reason.

Many priests compensate for this by the way they carry-out their leadership role in the Mass, but, equally, many others simply fall into the trap of reciting the prayers like an automaton, as though the prayers are some kind of formula which automatically brings about a certain action.[25] Many Catholics know priests who 'say' Mass as though they had a train to catch. They are experiencing, even today, of merely being present at what only amounts to a recitation of a formula of words and actions which they need not understand or to which they can relate. It is as though they need not really be involved but simply to be a witness of what is happening at

---

25 Official doctrine (see "Catechism" 1127) expressed in the Latin as "ex opere operato" i.e. by the fact of the actions performed, and not affected by the moral state of the priest, has caused much controversy.

the altar. What does it mean for us when we are told that the celebration of the Mass is the central act of worship in the life of the Church? What should it mean if our image of God is that revealed by Christ? If we are to be really honest to that image of God, is the present liturgy of the Mass, in its words and actions, true worship in spirit and truth?

"Through him, with him, and in him"

I have often wondered whether our attention has been diverted from the central importance of this prayer in the Mass by the emphasis on tying the validity of the sacrificial element to priestly office. As I propose in the next chapter on 'Priesthood', the priest's role has become so central to the Mass that the purpose of the people gathering in one place to offer themselves and their thanks to God (sacrifice), in that dynamic communion with Christ's death and resurrection, has become subordinate to a ritual of cultic priestly sacrifice at an altar. One result of this is that it is almost impossible to talk about the meaning of a Eucharistic service, particularly in the Catholic Mass, unless it is in the context of the role of the ordained priest. To try and justify my proposal that the central purpose of a celebration of the Eucharist is the movement towards 'koinonia', that dynamic union of faith and life with Christ 'through him, with him, and in him', without considering the reality of the control explicit in the cult of the ordained priest, would not be sensible under the present circumstances. This is why I have put together my thoughts on the Eucharist in the next chapter on "priesthood".

Vatican II – moving on?

Although much has changed since the Council of Vatican II, the underlying theological fault lines of the form and content of worship in the Mass, inherited from early Roman and medieval times, still produce such a distorted understanding of first, the image of God, and second, the meaning and purpose of the commemoration of Jesus' last supper. In identifying these 'fault lines' there is the danger of entering into a deep discussion where traditional theological language can obscure the essential focus. Having gone through years of studying the various 'schools' of theology and come out the other end with my sanity intact (I think!), I am well aware of the fact that I can never say that I have a full understanding of all the issues surrounding worship at Mass. However, in this attempt to be honest to God, I am trying to get behind the words to the root of their meaning, and at the same time to relate this to our present time and culture. This is what Pope John XXIII called "aggiornamento", bringing the Church up to date,[26] together with "resourcement", a return to the sources.

What does the Council of Vatican II mean for Catholic worship today? I am sure the majority of Catholics would have a hard time thinking of an answer. It all depends on our age. I was a 22 year old student 'testing a vocation' to the Catholic priesthood when the Council opened in 1962, at the time when Pope John XXIII was trying to 'open the doors' of the Church and let in some fresh air. I can remember the excitement and anticipation at the seminary that something momentous was beginning for the Church.

For those under 50 years of age it will be hard to appreciate just how significant the Council was for the 'people of God'. Even the Council's emphasis on that title for the members of

---

26 "Gaudet Mater Ecclesia" Pope's speech at opening of Vat.II 1962.

the world-wide Church was a sign of John's vision of updating and return to the sources. However, after over 50 years, it is generally recognised that the Council's teachings have not yet been fully assimilated into the life of the Church. At the time, the influential theologian, Karl Rahner, made the observation that the Council was "the beginning of the beginning". There have been many 'beginnings' but there is still much to be done before we can say that the legacy of the Council has been fully received and implemented, and what is more important, moving on to new understandings.

Less than a 100 days after his election in 1959, Pope John announced to the Church that he was calling an Ecumenical Council, 89 years after the first Vatican Council. This was great surprise to many and more of a nasty shock to those in the Church who were already complaining about the direction it was taking in the years preceding the announcement. The title of the fourth document produced by the Council "The Church in the Modern World", expresses what the Council was really all about. Whether it is the liturgy, the word of God in the Scriptures, the nature of the Church, and its mission to the world, the life of the Church can only take place in the context of the world *as it is today,* not as it was 89 years ago or 500 years ago. The Church, to be effective in its mission to the world, must constantly be brought up to date. At the same time, this updating must always be based on, must have its roots in, the Tradition of the Church. Not the many 'traditions' which it had accrued in its history, however valuable they may have been at one time, but the handing-on of the essential sources of the Christian faith: *"The centrality of Christ" – the Council is invoked to bear witness to this truth to the contemporary world."*[27]

---

27   Pope John XXII "Gaudet Mater Ecclesia" address to the Council.

Reform of communal worship

The reception at parish level of the Council's teachings has almost entirely been experienced in the context of worship in the liturgy of the Western Church, for this is where Catholics as a gathered community have traditionally experienced being 'Church'. The changes that were made related first of all to the liturgy, for its 'reform and promotion' was decided at the Council to be the most urgent task. The first paragraph of the Council's document on the liturgy set the tone and focus for all the others:

"The sacred Council has set out to impart an ever increasing vigour to the Christian life of the faithful; to adapt more closely to the needs of our age those institutions which are subject to change; to foster whatever can promote union among all who believe in Christ; to strengthen whatever can help to call all mankind into the Church's fold. Accordingly it sees particularly cogent reasons for undertaking the reform and promotion of the liturgy." [28]

We can see in that paragraph those elements of Pope John's vision for the Council – strengthening, adapting, uniting, reforming, and promoting the life of the Church. Very soon after the Council closed, we started to see and experience changes to the liturgy which enabled us to begin to participate in the liturgical life of the Church as full members of the 'Body of Christ'. It is no flight of fancy to equate the 'event' of the Council with the bursting of a mighty dam. The 'living water', the Spirit-filled life of the Church, had been held back by the building of 'dams', some small, some big, forming obstacles to Christ's work of bringing his "water of life" (John 4:14) to everyone. Individuals, sections and groupings, leaders and

---

28   The Constitution on the Sacred Liturgy "Sacrosanctum Concilium" 1963."Vatican II" Ed. Austin Flannery, O.P.

powerful officials from various parts of the Church were responsible for creating these 'dams', mainly because, in their blindness to Christ's teachings, they were misled into thinking that updating equated with error. At the same time, there were also those who built such 'dams' in order to hold onto their positions of power. It could be said that the Council burst many of those 'dams' but there has been a strong rearguard action by those wanting to reverse the progress since the Council and return to an authoritarian system of power and control in which any updating is regarded as a weakening of the Church's tradition.

There have been calls for a new Council in order that the many issues which have arisen since the end of Vatican II be explored at a universal level. Despite some headway being made on the subject of worship in the liturgy of the Church, the bishops at Vatican II did not really come to grips with the historical fault lines of the tradition formed around the role and authority of 'pastors', culminating in the control of worship being formally invested in a cultic priesthood. If worship is to be a service of devotion to God, through Christ, with Christ, and in Christ, both in the way we live our lives and also in our eucharistic gatherings, then a true conversion will have to take place in the minds of those leaders who have been trained to think only in terms of protecting the status quo through priestly control. That conversion can only come through the realisation that the freedom to worship 'in spirit and truth' is the gift of Christ's own sacrifice on the Cross, his triumph over death, his return to the Father, and his presence on Earth through the Holy Spirit. Any attempt to restrict that freedom ignores the importance of Christ's teachings about worship upon which all liturgical practices should be developed. Unfortunately, our freedom to worship 'in spirit and truth' has been largely surrendered to the imposition of forms and structures by an institution which encloses that 'service to God', under the control of a cultic priestly brotherhood. This situation begs the question as to whether this is in harmony with the Gospel or in fact is the consequence of the growth of a theology which put more trust in the cult of sacerdotal priesthood for such service to God than that initiated by Christ as the new "way, truth and life".(John 14:6)

Priesthood

As a result of a reactionary resistance to reform, the progress towards a true understanding of 'worship' in the liturgy, and therefore an image of God revealed by Jesus Christ, has slowed almost to a standstill. This is largely due to the resistance to any change in the theology of the priesthood of the people of God and that of the ordained priest as a mediator of that priesthood. Until the leaders of our Church embrace the consequences of the fundamental teaching about Christ revealing the image of God as 'our Father', together with the fundamental teaching about Christ being our 'High Priest', our only mediator of our access to God,[29] then the form of our 'worship', our devotion to God, will not be 'in spirit and truth', or indeed be honest to God.

What are these fault lines in relation to 'worship' at Mass? I have already noted the problem of language, in the way we approach and address God in neo-pagan terminology. How this has come about can only be explored by an expert church historian, but, nevertheless, it can be seen through a moderate study of church history that the close relationship that existed at times between the Church and State, particularly with the Roman Empire, led to a certain syncretism of ideas in expression of language and culture. Of course, it cannot be forgotten that

---

29 "Letter to the Hebrews" Chapters 8-9.

Christianity developed from the Jewish culture and milieu during the period of the early Church, and the language and culture of the Jewish people in the centuries before Christ heavily influenced the culture of the Christian Church after Christ. In both of these cultures, the language and practices of 'altar' sacrifice figured prominently in the religious rites, and despite the destruction of the Temple in Jerusalem by the Romans in 70 AD, the beliefs behind such practices continued in Judaism and of course in the Roman pagan cult. These influences on what became known as 'Roman Catholicism' can be clearly seen in the development of its liturgical practices around the altar at its central act of 'worship' at the Mass. It is as though Jesus' teachings about worship, both to the woman at the well (see above) and his identification of himself as the new 'Temple' where mercy replaces cultic sacrifices,[30] were relegated in favour of reverting to practices of altar sacrifice in order to express the commemoration of the Last Supper and Jesus' personal sacrifice on the Cross. In doing so, they also adopted practices of ritual, priestly cult and dress from the Roman state, with which we are so familiar today. This led to what can only be called a 'priestly caste' where uniformed men are ordained into a particular form of life and service which is closed to the rest of the people of God.

Altar sacrifice – a denial of the New Covenant?

The question on which I have long pondered is: did Jesus' sacrifice on the cross do away with 'altar sacrifice'? If this is the case, then is not the use of an altar at Mass by a priest a rejection of that fact? Was not that sacrifice of Jesus, that

---

30 Matthew 12:1-8; also Paul in 1Corinthians 3:9, 2 Cor.6:16, Ephesians 2:19-22, John 2:18-20.

'giving-up' of himself to the Father, making possible through his resurrection the beginning of a new human relationship for us, a new 'covenant', with God? Did this not make the practice of sacrifice at any kind of altar redundant, and in fact a denial of that new personal relationship?

The concept and language of offering sacrifices at an 'altar' was very much part of the religious life of the Israelites and also many of the other world religions e.g. the religious cults of the Greek and Roman empires. Historians have identified the origins of 'altar' sacrifice and its persistence throughout history but when the origins of 'sacrifice' itself are sought these are lost in the 'mist of times'. My focus here is on the persistence of 'priestly mediation' in Christian churches even though it appears that Jesus' own sacrifice fulfilled and completed the old teachings and workings of the Law. Access to God had been mediated through the high priest of the Temple who offered the old sacrifices at the altar in the 'Holy of Holies' area of the building. But now there was no need for such 'altar' sacrifices, using animals and crops, for a new way of sacrifice was brought about by Jesus on the Cross giving his life up to God. From that one perfect sacrifice which made his resurrection possible, mankind has been given direct access to God. It was his resurrection and ascension into heaven which changed the whole nature of sacrifice and our access to God. In this new relationship, access to God is no longer mediated through the priests and rituals of the old Law, but through Jesus Christ as Lord of Heaven and Earth. In the language of New Testament times he is the new perfect "high priest" who, as our "forerunner", has made it possible for us also to enter that new life which he has with his Father in Heaven.[31]

If Jesus is the sole mediator of our access to God and the promise of new life after death, and therefore changed the

---

31 NT "Letter to the Hebrews"4:14, 6:20.

nature of sacrifice in our acts of 'worship', why are there priests offering Jesus' sacrifice at an altar in the ritual of the Mass? Even though Catholics are taught that the Mass is a 're-presentation' or enactment of Jesus' once-and-for-all sacrifice on the cross, nevertheless the mediation of a priest at an altar, in language and in fact, in effect denies that change in access to God . If it was a true commemoration as Christ asked at his last supper, then we would be talking about a 'table' and a 'meal' and not an altar with all that signifies. Many books, talks, sermons and official teachings have been produced about the theology of 'the sacrifice of the Mass', and I have read and studied tomes produced by the so-called 'schools' of theology on this and related subjects. Even though at times in my life I accepted the official teachings on this particular subject, nevertheless there was always the nagging thought that they didn't match up with my understanding of the New Testament teachings. It is not that I disagree with all that has been taught but that, if I am really honest, I find the conclusions unconvincing in the light of the NT teachings, particularly those expounded in the "Letter to the Hebrews". As time has gone on I have become more convinced that by putting the idea of 'the sacrifice of the Mass' at the centre of this commemoration of 'the Lord's Supper', the new era of access to God, brought about by Jesus for these 'end times', has been obscured by a layer of ritual which once again uses altar sacrifice through priestly mediation.

I mentioned above that "The Letter to the Hebrews" has had a significant influence on the development of my views. It is not one of the favoured letters of the NT, mainly because it contains a lot of teaching from the OT, and also because some passages can be difficult to understand if you are not familiar with biblical theology. Yet, there are very significant teachings which shed light on the foundations of Christianity. Ever since I had to study it in depth for my formal studies, I have frequently turned to it for help in moving on in my 'faith seeking understanding'.

If there is one letter in the NT which points to the teaching on the new way for our access to God and therefore provides the foundations for understanding that there is now only one 'priest', one mediator for that access, in the person of Jesus Christ our Lord, it is this letter. The question of how and why these teachings have either been ignored or interpreted to give another meaning by those holding high office in the Church would be worth exploring by theologian/historians. One internationally respected professor of New Testament studies, James D.G. Dunn, confesses the same bewilderment *"at the way the argument of Hebrews can be so lightly ignored or set aside by those Christian traditions which wish to continue to justify a special order of priesthood within the people of God, a special order whose priestly ministry is distinct in kind from the priesthood of all the faithful."*[32] The historical fact that the existence of priestly mediation in the Church's practices of 'worship' is evidence of such an interpretation, tends to suggest that somewhere along the line of history other factors took precedence over the teachings of this letter, even though it became part of the 'canon' of Scripture. The importance of this letter, within the context of the whole of the New Testament, for the purposes of seeking a true understanding of 'priesthood' and our access to God cannot be exaggerated.

The perfect mediator of access to God

The author of the letter, which was probably composed during the last quarter of the first century AD, describes Jesus as the perfect mediator for our access to God and the promised new life, because as 'the Son of God' and the 'son of man' he is able to have 'solidarity' with us and therefore is *"a compassionate*

---

32 "The Partings of the Ways" 2nd edition, p.127.

and trustworthy high priest for their relationship to God" (2:17). Having overcome death and ascended to Heaven, he is the only person through and in whom we are able to enter into that new life. He is, therefore, the only mediator between us and God the Father. The old priesthood is no longer necessary, for Jesus becomes the new way of direct access to the Father. In the language of 1st century Judeo/Christian culture, he is the new 'High Priest' for that access. In addition to this revelation, the other authors of the New Testament, particularly Paul and John, made the important point that even though Jesus was in Heaven as the perfect mediator, his gift of his Spirit fulfils his promise that he would always be with us on earth.

Access to God through a sacerdotal priesthood?

What did this mean for those early Christians? In their devotion (worship) to Jesus did they believe in this access to God through the ascended ('exalted') Jesus or did they find it difficult to break with the old traditions of the Levitical priesthood if they were Jews, and the pagan priesthood if they were Gentiles? Much has been written about this even though there is relatively little evidence other than which can be read in the later Epistles and Luke's "Acts of the Apostles" of the New Testament. However, it can be said with some certainty that in the early years of the Church there was nothing in the faith practices of those Christians which remotely has any connection with a new priestly order where access to God's loving activity towards mankind (grace) is mediated through particular individuals offering sacrifice on behalf of the people, as there is today in the Mass.[33]

---

33   cf. Dunn, 109-110.

An early example of this is in the writings of Justin Martyr in about 155 AD, where he describes what the Christians do on "the day of the Sun" i.e. Sun-day. The simple structure of (a) a gathering of people, (b) readings from the apostles and prophets, (c) preaching by presider, (d) prayers of the people, (e) bread and wine brought forward, (f) prayers and thanksgivings over them by presider, (g) distribution and partaking of bread and wine, (h) portion sent to absent by deacons, (i) collection for those in need, is apparently typical of the communal service to God at that time.[34] The role of 'presider' did not have anything to do with a sacerdotal priesthood but was to lead and facilitate the people's service to God and each other in a special assembly on the first day of the week which commemorated Christ's resurrection.

The new covenant's access to God does not mean the institution of a new priesthood, nor the creation of a ritual order, nor any kind of investiture.[35] It is clear from the few references in Luke's "Acts" and writings such as from Justin, that the focus of Christians' communal devotion was to do what Jesus asked or commanded at his last supper, which was to commemorate his actions, that is, to bring to mind in a real re-enactment, what he did at that Passover supper. The essential point here is that this did not require a human priest to do this, for Jesus himself had made it possible for them to be in communion (koinonia) with his own sacrifice and triumph over death through such a meal. In that meal, it is the Spirit of Jesus which brings about that communion with Jesus in the eating of the bread and the drinking of the wine. It is important to remember that it is the eating and drinking, the taking into ourselves the bread and wine, which is the central point of

---

34   "The First Apology of Justin" in "The Ante-Nicene Fathers" vol.I, p.186.
35   Dom Sebastian Moore "The Secular Implications of Liturgy" in "The Christian Priesthood", 9th Downside Symposium, 1970.

the meal. Jesus becomes present not to be adored or to receive adulation, but to unite himself to those who 'take him in to themselves' through that meal. This has an important relevance to the practices of 'worship' connected with the Mass which we are so familiar with today.

Access to God through Christ

Jesus inaugurated a new kind of 'worship', one in which *everyone* will have direct and intimate access to God. Prior to this, the people of God could only have such access mediated through the priests of the Temple who offered sacrifices and prayers on their behalf. This is not to say that the people did not have *any* kind of access to God. They were able to hear the word of God in the readings of the Scriptures and through the mouths of their prophets and teachers, and were able to respond in prayer and to worship God through their obedience to the Commandments.

But to have a deeply personal and immediate access to the very presence of God was not possible. The 'sacred', the divine domain, was separate from their everyday life and was controlled and supervised by the priests of the Temple, who were withdrawn from a particular section of the community. The people were taught that the 'presence' of God dwelt in the Holy of Holies of the Temple in Jerusalem, the same divine presence which dwelt in a movable tabernacle, the Ark of the Covenant, which they carried with them when they were nomadic people on their long journeys to the Promised Land. Access to the Holy of Holies could only be made by the high priest who entered there once a year through a veil which separated that place from the rest of the Temple. The apostle Matthew made reference to this veil which, as a result of an earthquake at the death of

Jesus, was "rent in two". (27:51) What significance is this for our own access to God?

The tearing-open of the veil at Christ's death signified that the way to personal access to God was no longer closed to the people but is at all times and in every place now open. The Son of God himself becomes the 'High Priest' giving us access to God the Father: *"We have then, brethren, complete confidence through the blood of Jesus in entering the sanctuary by a new way he has opened for us through the curtain, that is, through his flesh."*[36] Jesus has entered the heavenly sanctuary, our ultimate "rest"[37] with God, as the "forerunner" (pioneer, pathfinder) of our access to that new life. Now there is no need for earthly altars and sanctuaries for a cultic priest to act on behalf of the people, for Christ has changed the nature and place of sacrifice and worship. It is only in the heavenly sanctuary, the true sanctuary, that Christ's mediation takes place *"in the presence of God"*.[38]

With these early house-gatherings for the celebration of the Last Supper, the only 'priesthood' necessary was in Jesus' own position 'at the right hand of God' to mediate their access to God. We do not know how much these early Christians understood what was happening but they were only concerned to do what Jesus had asked them to do. In this way, they must have been conscious of their union with Jesus and with each other, drawing spiritual strength from that communion, through taking-in the life of Jesus in the bread and wine.

---

36 Hebrews. 10:20
37 Ibid. 4:1-11.
38 Ibid. 9:24.

The return to a cultic priesthood

How did it come about that from such an act of 'worship' we now experience the celebration of Jesus' Last Supper once again mediated through a priestly order with all the connotations and historical accretions which necessarily come from such a focus? I do not want to enter into a comprehensive study of the history of this development for that would only make this essay become an academic historical work rather than keeping its focus on the consequences of the distorted image of God. However, there are one or two facts which are important to consider when looking back to the sources of our present practices and doctrines concerning priesthood and how this has affected our image of God and therefore our 'worship'.

The first point is there is no evidence that the notion that all Christians share in a 'common priesthood' was uppermost in the minds of those early Christians who met to celebrate and commemorate Jesus' Last Supper. Indeed, the terms 'priesthood' and 'priest' were still associated with the Judaism or paganism with which they were familiar. How much they were aware of Peter and Paul's letters and therefore their respective teachings about that "priesthood" of all believers is hard to say. What is clear is that the title of 'priest' was not used to designate any particular office within the Christian community of the Ist century.[39] They soon realised that leaders and organisers were required for the growing movement but these were given the designation of 'elders' (Gk.presbuteroi), not because of their age but probably chosen for their experience and wisdom: *"In each of these churches they appointed elders, and with prayer and fasting they commended them to the Lord in*

---

39   Dunn, "In all the references to Christian worship and Christian community within the NT, there is simply no allusion to any order of priesthood within the Christian congregations." P.122.

whom they had come to believe." (Acts.14:23) It is interesting to note that this 'appointing' bears no meaning which relates to the practice of sacramental ordination which was attached to the later appointment of priests in the Roman wing of the universal Church. It appears that it was a simple matter of the Christian groups choosing the right persons to be their guides and mentors. If there was a 'laying of hands' on those chosen, this was a sign of their blessing and a sign of the work of the Holy Spirit for a particular role in the community.[40]

It wasn't until about the beginning of the 4th century that the Old Testament language of 'priesthood' with all its connotations, coupled with the rituals and practices of pagan Rome, began the process of conferring sacral status to those chosen as 'presbyters'. From that time, the development of a priestly 'order', particularly with the subsequent alliance of the Christian Church with the Roman state, gathered momentum to such an extent that virtually all 'worship' once again became mediated through the actions and words of individual 'priests'. Significantly, at the same time, since the destruction of the Temple, Judaism itself had developed from its previous focus on priestly mediation and temple worship to that of rabbinic teaching. It can be said that where Christian office-holders were leading the Church into the central focus of priestly mediation and cultic ritual sacrifice, much of Judaism was at the same time moving away from such priestly ritual to that of the teaching ministry.[41] Also it can be said that had the Christian Church not moved to the return of a priestly cult separate from the priesthood of the people but retained its central focus on the teaching ministry, perhaps the later divisions between Jew and Gentile may not have been so sharply drawn. Also, such a development could have prevented the later divisions in

---

40   Acts.8:17-18
41   Dunn pp.336-337.

the Christian movement and also the unjustified teachings of Christian leaders concerning the Jews which were only partially corrected at Vatican II.

Sacrifice- giving ourselves to God

The present-day title and function of 'priest' given to those chosen to be the leaders of Christian communities today is therefore not derived from the original Christian tradition, and what is more important, it represents a false understanding of our access to God the Father and a false understanding of the NT references to 'sacrifice of praise'[42] and 'spiritual sacrifices'[43] which have nothing to do with priestly sacrifice at an altar. Starting from the idea of sacrifice being 'the giving up to God', these spiritual sacrifices are manifested through our perseverance in living the Christian life. Through that witness to Jesus we are giving 'praise' to God the Father. Not the praise of adulation, but acknowledging God as the creator of all the good that is done in our words and actions and which demonstrate our union with his Son in and through their Spirit. Our communal acts of 'worship' then become the time to express our devotion, our thanks, and our union with each other through a special union with Jesus in our eating the 'bread of life' at the commemoration of his Last Supper. This 'giving up to God' of ourselves is the only 'sacrifice' which God asks of us. It is then that we unite ourselves to Jesus' sacrifice on the Cross and which brings about our at-one-ment with God the Father. As can be seen, this does not require a person other than Christ to mediate this loving action of God (grace), so do we need anyone to mediate our response?

---

42 Hebrews 13:15.
43 1Peter 2:4-5.

Leaders and guides?

It is a fact of human life that we all need leaders and guides in the many activities in which we take part. The Church is, therefore, no exception. It was necessary that Jesus chose those helpers who were to spread his message of the Good News (Gospel) to the rest of the world; he was, after all, fully human and at that time couldn't be in many places at once. Later, of course, after his resurrection and ascension, his presence and power was everywhere because of the gift of his Spirit. Yet, because of the great gift of human freedom at the time of the beginning of 'Creation', however long that took in human terms of time and space, it was necessary that the Holy Spirit works in and through human persons without compromising that freedom. That gift of absolute freedom was to make possible the freedom to love. We need to be reminded again and again that love can only be true love when it is absolutely free.

Jesus' example of leadership

We need human leaders and guides, but do we need them to control or govern our access to God? What was Jesus' example of leadership? Throughout the four Gospels, which are the only sources recorded about the way Jesus went about his mission, it can be seen that his whole approach was one of attraction, not coercion. Preaching his message of 'the truth' about his Father, about his Father's love for mankind and all creation, showing in his own actions of compassion and love how we should respond in the way we relate to him and each other, Jesus *attracted* people to that message. In this way people were motivated to respond freely to the attractiveness of God's love and truth in the person and word of Jesus. Today, the Holy Spirit, as the Spirit of truth and love, brings to our spirits the immediacy of God's love and truth revealed in his Son, Jesus Christ. However, our spirit can only respond through the actual reality of human nature. It is how we show that truth and love in the world in which we live that we demonstrate the attractiveness of Jesus' message. If our leaders and guides, whether they are called priests or pastors or some other title, abandon their primary task of teaching the attractiveness of the Gospel message and resort to authoritarian methods of control rather than leadership, then they become whom Jesus called the "blind guides".[44]

How does this compare to what we experience in the Church today? Are we attracted or repelled by the attitude and actions of those who are meant to be our leaders and guides? Is it the way they exercise their office or is it the office itself and its message which either attracts or repels? There is no doubt that many people have become estranged from the Church through the appalling attitude of some priests or through a bad personal experience which has left them with a deep feeling of resentment, not only against that particular priest but also against the institution. Others have been repelled by an authoritarian manner of both individual priests and senior office-holders of the institution. However, there are pastors who, in spite of the shortcomings of the institution and its traditions, attract people to the Christian message and way of life by their adoption of Jesus' example in their attitude and relationships with others. These men, and unfortunately only men in the Roman Catholic Church, are 'beacons of light' working within institutional rules and structures which tend to stifle the work of the Holy Spirit. I have met and worked alongside these true pastors who through their word and witness, not their duties as a priest, have strengthened my own faith and perseverance. At the present time of writing, my concern is that more and more

---

44 Matt.15:14, 23:16-24.

of newly ordained priests appear to place priority on those ideas and practices of cultic ritual rather than their prime function of giving witness to the Gospel.[45]

The sacralisation of order

One such 'structure' which has been at the centre of the debate about leading and guiding is the 'order of priests' in the Christian Church. There has been so much sacralisation and superstitious sacerdotalism surrounding this development in the history of the Church from the 'presbyter' to the 'priest', that it is no wonder that this 'office' took on the very form of that priestly mediation which was replaced by Jesus. Theoretically, it is said that the ordained priest does not mediate but facilitates our personal access to God. In other words, he is there to represent the gathered community to God the Father, and to represent Jesus Christ to the community. However, whichever way you look at it, in practice the priest stands between the people and God, as the 'go-between'. The history of the Church shows that this development from those chosen to be pastors, leaders and guides, to becoming controllers of the 'grace' of God, is a result of the failure of these 'leaders' to keep their focus firmly on the example of Jesus.

Controlling forgiveness

This is even more pronounced in the control exercised by priests over the 'sacramental life' of the Church. I do not want to get into the whole theology of what the Catechism calls 'the sacramental economy'; that is for another day. However, in this

---

45 Hebrews 13:7.

context of the role of priests, there are seven official sacraments over which the priest has some control. One of these, called 'the sacrament of reconciliation', or the practice of 'confession', particularly epitomises the development of priestly control over the lives of Catholics. If there is one particular practice in the Church which has not only distorted Jesus' teaching on forgiveness but has driven many away from the Church, it is this one. Why is that so? Did not Jesus say to his disciples that whose sins they forgive are forgiven, and whose sins they retain they are retained?[46] Biblical scholars have argued about the authenticity of this particular text, especially the fact that this is not recorded in the other three earlier gospels, but that is not the problem for those Catholics who do not go to 'confession' any more. What is abhorrent to most of them is the meaning and form of the practice which moved away from Jesus' teachings about forgiveness. Throughout Jesus' teachings there are numerous instances of individuals being told by Jesus that their sins are forgiven, and what is central in these cases is that Jesus joined such forgiveness to the person's faith in Jesus himself as the Son of God. That authority to forgive sins is in God alone. How the Church's leaders and guides interpreted and understood how this works in practice is symptomatic of how they see their role as pastors of God's love for his people.

The 'grace' of God, that is his loving action, is not some *thing* which can be manipulated or controlled by those chosen to be our pastors. Whatever our understanding is about our pastors' and office-holders' *authority* to facilitate our reconciliation with God after committing 'serious' or 'mortal' sins, it is the form of the practice of 'confession' which has turned Catholics away from it and very often from the Church itself. Much has already been written about the terrible experiences of many people 'going to confession', as it is still commonly called, in

---

46 John 20:23.

seeking relief from their feelings of guilt. Looking at it from my own personal experience and understanding, I now believe that the reason for its existence and prominence in the life of the Catholic Church is based not only on a false understanding of one particular text, but what is more important, on a false image of Jesus' teachings about forgiveness.

Tight control of a process

This is not to say that many of the official teachings do not contain some true understanding of forgiveness, but there is a yawning gap between the theory and practice of its meaning and action which suggests there are serious faults in those doctrines. It is Jesus' teachings of forgiveness *in action,* how it is practiced in everyday life, which is the example to follow if we are to understand its importance in our relationship to God and each other. To put that example of forgiveness into the 'straightjacket' of the official rules governing the theory and practice of the 'sacrament of reconciliation' is symptomatic of the control inevitably exercised by the development of priestly mediation.

We are all aware that once you have created a system where control is exercised by persons bound by vows of obedience, then the rules themselves can take on an importance out of proportion to the purpose of the system. If, at the same time, the system itself is based on a faulty premise, then the rules themselves are devised from an unsound base. An example of this in the practice of 'confession' to a priest is, first of all, the requirement to seek forgiveness from God through the mediation of a priest who performs a prescribed ritual in order that a sacramental action of reconciliation with God may take place. Instead of a pastor leading and guiding the members of his community to an understanding of forgiveness, there is tight control of a process.

Within that process there is the rule governing the practical implications of the teaching on 'penance' with the imposition by the priest of 'appropriate' penances for the penitent. This is an example of where a particular rule is based on a faulty understanding of Jesus' teachings in the NT, in this case on 'repentance', which means 'turning away' from sin to a new way of life. Somehow, there developed in the Church the notion of performing 'acts of penance' to show repentance and in the case of serious sins to be part of the 'process' of restoring 'grace' to the soul. What is more, these 'penances' often take on the form of having to recite certain well known prayers in repetitive form e.g. the 'Hail Mary' and 'Glory be to the Father'. What a distortion of the whole meaning of prayer, to use it as a penance! These distortions of Jesus' teachings on his Father's loving forgiveness and our response is a result of the development of 'authority' in the Church as power and control through priestly office rather than authority through teaching truth. (I will refer to the well-known texts where Peter and the other apostles are given authority to 'bind and loose' in the next chapter on 'authority'.)

To interpret Jesus' teachings on forgiveness by developing the form and content of a ritual which in practice has turned away countless people from the Church and what is more create a barrier for many to access 'the bread of life' in the Eucharist, is once more a symptom of the distorted image of God prevalent in the Church today. Throughout Jesus' teachings and actions in relation to forgiveness, the one requirement was for people to have faith in him and to have the desire to turn away from sin. He required no structured ritual but simply a change of heart and mind which led them to have faith in him, and also enabled them to forgive others. To have a way, structured or not, for helping people to have that faith in Jesus, that change of heart and mind, and therefore seek forgiveness and to forgive others is one of the central duties of a pastor, provided that 'way' is the way of Jesus which will always attract and not deter. The fact that the form and content of the 'sacrament of reconciliation' has deterred many is indicative of it not being the right way to bring people to the attractiveness of 'the way, the truth and the life'.

The precious gift of freedom

The idea that the sacramental life of the Church can only be available through the mediation of priests is yet another example of the authoritarian control which developed from the clericalisation of those offices of the Church which were originally meant to be at the service of the people's freedom to 'worship in spirit and truth'. This notion of freedom is so important in the context of the Church but even more so in the context of God's self-communication in the person of Jesus his Son, that it has been a subject which has hugely influenced my own understanding of God's action (grace) in our lives.

One of the reasons that many people are either deterred from accepting the existence of the Christian God in the first place, or have lost their once-held belief in such a God, is that they cannot accept that the Christian God will allow the suffering and 'evil' which they see around them. In my conversations with Christians and non-Christians alike, this has become a stumbling block despite being attracted by other Christian teachings. It hasn't helped that the standard response from the clergy is one where suffering becomes, in theological technical language, a 'mystery', and something which can in fact lead us to faith through offering such suffering to God. Whatever truths may be in that response, there is little attempt to propose that God's gift of freedom to Creation, together with giving mankind the responsibility to care for Creation in that freedom, created the possibility that imperfect man could abuse that freedom and cause much of the suffering around us. This does not explain everything about suffering but perhaps it focusses on what we can do, rather than just accepting suffering as a 'fait accompli'.

Apart from any philosophical arguments for the existence of God, Christians accept that Jesus Christ, in his person and word, is God's self-communication. If we accept Jesus' teachings that love is at the very centre of our relation to God and each other, then for that love to be true it has to be free. By that created gift of freedom we have a certain amount of autonomy over our lives, but it also creates in us a certain vulnerability, which the story of Adam and Eve illustrates. Such freedom generates responsibility for our actions which may or may not be good for mankind and the world. The existence of suffering in the world may well be the result of the misuse of that freedom, not only in human relationships but also in lack of care for the world around us.

For us to be able to love God and show love to each other, there can be no compromise on that freedom to love by not having the freedom not to love. We are either free or we are not; there is no halfway house here. In God's wisdom, in his plan for our fulfilment, he protects that gift of complete freedom by attraction, not coercion. This attractiveness of the truth about God and about ourselves, revealed in Jesus, is presented to us to respond in freedom.

However, because of that freedom, there is always the possibility that it can be used to restrict one another's freedom. When I was teaching for a short while at a large Catholic comprehensive school, I demonstrated this seeming paradox by getting a student to stand on a particular spot in the classroom. I then asked another student to stand on the same spot. Of course, this was impossible if the first student didn't move. I then asked the class to think about the fact that if each had the freedom to stand on that spot, how can that freedom be fulfilled in practice? There was the usual suggestion of enforcing that freedom by pushing one out of the way, but the suggestion of asking the first student to step away from the spot to allow the other student to exercise his freedom soon became their answer. This demonstrated that our right to express freedom is sometimes something to freely give up in a spirit of sacrificial love for each other, but at no time is that freedom to love compromised. As the many stories from the World War II concentration camps show, despite the huge deprivations and sufferings of the inmates, many were able to demonstrate, sometimes in very small ways, that freedom to express love to others in the only way they could.

Ministers as enforcers.

What does this show about our freedom to 'worship in spirit and truth' in the context of the Church and its ministers? How have our leaders and guides protected that freedom from coercion about which Irenaeus, one of the early Fathers of the Church, taught that man's free will was not compromised by God's action (grace)? *"For all these sayings (Christ's teachings) set forth the free will of man, and how God is a counsellor to us, exhorting us to submit to him, and turning us aside from disobeying him, but not using any compulsion."*[47] The history of the Church shows that this understanding of the relationship between freedom and truth, between freedom and grace, between freedom and worship, became subsumed under the weight of a new kind of slavery to laws and regulations. In human terms, where there is a system of laws there is inevitably

---

47 "Against the Heresies" Book IV, ch.xxxvii.3.

those who have to enforce them. In the case of the Church, the 'enforcers' were those very ministers who were appointed and commissioned to be leaders and guides in preaching the Gospel. This form of control became firmly developed in the clericalisation of the Church, where these ministers became enforcers of church law, governing the lives of the people in the development from the Commemoration of Christ's Last Supper to 'The Sacrifice of the Mass' and many other sacramental actions in the life of the Church, as well as a myriad of rules and regulations relating to the 'moral life'.

This changeover from pastor to priest, from 'table-fellowship' to a system of church law which controls an elaborate ritual of priestly sacrifice, from the practice of forgiveness to a ritual of priestly mediation, from freedom to worship in spirit and truth to a complicated system of control enforced with sanctions, has produced the situation where Jesus' actions in freeing us to worship in spirit and truth has been compromised in the search for complete control. The reasons for this are many and varied and includes those times when 'government' of the Church became the same as the government of a State, with all the implications and trappings of such a development, of the thirst for power and privilege, of wealth and prestige, of self- importance and titles. A complete contrast to the principles and teachings of the Gospel. In the Church today, we are still experiencing some of the consequences of those disastrous times.

Graced freedom

Like many others, I have wrestled with this notion of human freedom, especially when I have experienced the many limitations on that freedom in everyday life. To say that I am free in the sense of being able to do what I like is clearly an absurdity in the light of experience and also in the absurdity of denying the restrictions of time and space in the physical world in which I live. Yet, in the midst of such limitations in life, the freedom to love is unrestricted, provided we are not in such a physical and mental condition as to be unable to express it. If this is true, then how does the question of God's grace sit with this notion of freedom? Does God's gracious action in my life negate my freedom or does it protect it and enhance it?

The answer to this question, if there is a convincing one, is important in the context of our free will to worship in spirit and truth, and how pastors and church office-holders should care for and serve that freedom. St. Augustine of Hippo didn't get everything right (like all of us!), but he said many things which illuminate our understanding of our Christian faith. This is particularly so on this question of the relationship of our free will with God's action through his Spirit called 'grace'. The particular section of his teaching which is relevant starts with the assertion that God's gracious action towards us is to give us the ability to love that which is good *"but volition is in man's power"*.[48] In other words, even though the act of willing is my own act, it is God who gives me the ability to will only that which is good. But how can it be said that my will is truly free if God makes it possible for me to will *only* that which is good? This is what he replies *"This will (to believe) is to be ascribed to the divine gift, not merely because it arises from our free will, which was created naturally with us, but also because God acts upon us <u>by the incentives of our perceptions,</u> to will and to believe, either by external evangelical exhortations.... or internally where no man has in his control what shall enter his thoughts, although it appertains to his own free will to consent or dissent"*. (my underlining) In other words, we are attracted by what we perceive as the truth revealed by God and this

---

48 "On the Spirit and the Letter" ch.54

motivates us to freely accept it. If this was not true then there would be no need for preaching and teaching to convince us. God would simply manipulate us like puppets. To have faith in God requires us to believe he is who he is through belief in his self-communication in his Son and his gospel, the 'good news'. For such belief to be true and honest it has to be freely given.

What does this mean for the way that pastors and office-holders should approach the whole question of the believer's freedom to worship in spirit and truth? If their calling, their role in the Church, is to 'feed' and care for Christ's people (see John 21), then that care, that feeding, through preaching the Gospel, has to be done through the very attraction of the truth of the Gospel. The word of God in Jesus Christ attracts, does not compel; God does not negate his gift of free will. We are motivated by that attraction of truth which is revealed to us, and it is that which creates the need for pastors to preach the Gospel. Any attempt to control by coercion or sanction, by structures or office, by a system of laws and traditions, our freedom to worship in spirit and truth, is a misunderstanding of that relationship between grace and freedom.

Not seeing the wood for the trees

The development of the ordained priesthood as we see it today, with all the accretions gathered over hundreds of years, some good, some bad, has made the task of defining the essential role of those appointed to lead and guide the 'people of God' that much more difficult for them. The Jesuit theologian, Robert Murray attempted a definition of priesthood as a religious phenomenon which shows how similar it is to the function and status of today's Catholic priest in contrast to the original role of 'pastor' of God's people : *"A priest is a cult official recognised by a given religious group as having a mediatoral function and status with regard to the deity and to men, such that he is understood in some sense to act and speak for each to the other. The characteristic priestly activity is leading worship and especially performing sacrifice, often in a sanctuary to which priests have privileged access; such sacrifice, correctly performed, is understood to be acceptable to the deity and to win his favour for men."*[49]

Such a definition can be applied to the sacerdotal priesthood of the Christian Church as well as that of many pagan cultures, and easily leads to a cultic priestly brotherhood where privilege and status grows to such an extent that we see, even today, office-holders given such extravagant and inappropriate titles of address as 'Your Excellency', 'Your Eminence', 'My Lord Bishop', 'Most Reverent', 'Very Reverent', etc. To some this may seem not very important in the great scheme of things, but it is indicative of a mentality which is so foreign to that of the Gospel of Jesus Christ. Is such a state of mind and heart really reflecting the image of God? Are we being really 'honest to God' in accepting such a false face of Christian pastoral ministry?

Need for a different kind of ministry

Jesus' mandate to those chosen and appointed to lead, guide, feed and care for his 'flock' has been obscured by layers of duties and functions of a cultic priesthood to such an extent that the original role is no longer clearly seen and experienced by the people of God. This is not to say that many individual priests do not act in such a pastoral way, but if the theology and structures of a cultic priesthood inevitably lead to more value being placed on the priorities of correctly performing rites by

---

49   Art. "Christianity's 'Yes' to Priesthood" in "The Christian Priesthood" ed.N.Lash
       & J.R.Hymer. 1970.

a particular privileged person having a status within a priestly caste or brotherhood, then the ministry of a true pastor has to be separate from that which obscures the expressed will of Jesus Christ. This means that if the present form of the local pastor as a cultic priest is not likely to be reformed because of the persistence of its underlying historical, cultural and theological fault lines, then there is the possibility of pressure (from the Holy Spirit?) arising for a different kind of pastoral ministry outside of the existing structure.

This is not something new for the universal Christian movement. After the Reformation of the 16th century this was precisely what happened in some of the branches of the reformed churches, simply because of the refusal of the official leaders/controllers of the Roman Catholic Church to accept the idea that there was anything in the nature and functions of the Catholic priesthood which needed to be reformed if it was to be true to the will of Jesus Christ. As a result, today we have Christian church communities who do not have a cultic priesthood, instead they are ministered to by either ordained or appointed pastors and, unfortunately, have had to become separated from those institutions, such as the Roman Catholic one, in order to be able to express and practice that ministry. The Anglican Church has kept a substantial amount of the nature and practice of a cultic priesthood although rejecting certain theologies of sacrifice and the Eucharist,[50] albeit with differing views among some sections of that communion.

There is no doubt in my mind that if the leaders of the Church refuse to initiate a synodal gathering in which there are no limitations imposed on discussion about the nature and purpose of the sacerdotal priesthood in relation to the Gospel of Jesus Christ, not only will there be a continuing decline in genuine pastoral ministry but also the institutional

---

50   E.g. doctrines of the "sacrifice of the Mass" and "transubstantiation".

control of that free access to communion (koinonia) with Christ for all believers in the consuming of his life in the Eucharist will continue to fly in the face of God. For the sake of the Church there has to be recognition that Jesus Christ did not 'institute' such a priesthood, for the very important reason that a sacerdotal sacrificing priesthood was no longer necessary to mediate his people's access to God. His sacrifice, his giving-up of himself to his Father, fulfilled and completed all cultic sacrifices, making the only 'sacrifice' of praise and thanksgiving acceptable as our response. Any notion of continually offering to God the Father, Christ's sacrifice of himself through a priestly brotherhood, is a doctrine and practice which denies the radical nature of the change in our access to God and a lack of honesty to the Gospel. At the same time, it denies the fact that Christ changed the nature and place of worship which no longer is tied to a system of cultic ritual but is centred on that 'koinonia', that communion with Christ himself.

Authority to preach the Gospel or authority to govern?

This question about our freedom to worship in spirit and truth also brings in the question about 'authority'. What exactly is 'authority' in the context of Christianity and its Church and how is it expressed and practised by its pastors and office-holders? Is it a power to compel Christians to do certain things with corresponding sanctions or punishments if they do not comply, or is it a teaching authority presenting 'authentic' truths to be accepted or not accepted? What kind of authority is really being 'honest to God'?

Use and misuse of language

Yet again, we are faced with the language used by the leaders and pastors of the Church, and this was particularly important at the sessions on the Church at the Council of Vatican II (1961-65). Although there were efforts by a number of bishops and theologians to update the terminology of Christian doctrine in order to bring out the essential truths, the final document on the

Church "Lumen Gentium" (LG) still contains not only out of date language but also ambiguity in translation of the original Greek biblical texts when put into English. There is no doubt that much of this was due to those office-holders who simply used those terms which had been traditionally used and, in the context of 'authority', which perpetuated the monarchical notions of ruling and governing the 'People of God'. In giving some examples of this I am not inferring that this document on the Church has no value for continuing to "build-up the Body of Christ." There is much in it that, at the time, suggested progress in renewal and reform, but the office-holders of the institution had become so reliant on methods of control that this has stifled many changes needed for the good of the Church.

Guiding or ruling?

The following statement of the Council members is an example of where the notion of control persisted despite the efforts of theologians to return to the original New Testament teachings: "*This is the sole Church of Christ.........which our Saviour, after his resurrection, entrusted to Peter's pastoral care (Jn.21:17), commissioning him and the other apostles to extend and rule it (cf. Mtt. 28:18 etc.).*"[51] (my underlining). There is no reference to 'ruling' members of the Church in that New Testament reference: "*Go therefore and make disciples of all nations, baptizing them in the name of the Father and of the Son and of the Holy Spirit, teaching them to obey everything that I have commanded you.*" (my underlining). Why did the members of the Council refer to this text as their authority to rule the people of God? Were they simply following the

---

51 "Lumen gentium" 8 ("Vatican Council II. The Conciliar and Post Conciliar Documents" Gen.ed.Austin Flannery, 1975.)

traditional language reflecting the official understanding of their authority as the same as a civic ruler or monarch which, for example, was at its height at the time of the Papal States? They seemed to have ignored the fact that Jesus is emphasizing his disciples' commission as teachers, guides and carers, not rulers or governors.

The section in LG continues in this theme of 'control' when in the next paragraph we read that *"This Church.........which is <u>governed</u> by the successor of Peter and by the bishops in communion with him." (my underlining).* Throughout Jesus' teachings in the four gospels there is no suggestion that the leaders of his Church are to govern the people of God. This is an example of reading back into the New Testament something which is not there, purely and simply either to justify the status quo of the institution in present times or to maintain continuity with the language used by previous office-holders.

Even more explicit is this statement in the section on "the People of God" in the same document: *"The ministerial priest, by the sacred power that he has, forms and rules the priestly people;...."*[52] On which teaching of the Gospel of Jesus Christ is such a claim being made? If we attempt to fit this into any of Jesus' teachings and the subsequent teachings of the NT authors, it can only be done through a misunderstanding of the original meaning, i.e. of commissioning to guide and teach.

This control of the so-called 'lay-faithful' has been justified by the teaching that there has been handed down from Christ through the Apostles to the ordained ministers of today, the authority to 'rule' the People of God. Even at Vatican II, where there was a battle between those who could see the fault-lines of such teaching and those who wanted no change, this idea of clerics ruling the faithful still found its way in to other documents: *"Union with those whom the Holy*

---

52 Lumen gentium 10

Spirit has appointed to rule the Church of God is an essential element of the Christian apostolate."[53] *(my underlining).* This statement is supported with a reference, often quoted, from Luke's "Acts of the Apostles" 20:28, but the original Greek text uses the terms 'episcopous' which denotes overseers or guardians, and 'poimainein' denoting shepherds or pastors. Such terms were used in the New Testament to describe an office or position which is akin to protecting and guiding rather than any compulsion by a ruler. To say that the Holy Spirit appoints men to *rule* the people of God is a misreading of that text and does not reflect the focus of other texts such as, for example, in chapter 14 of John's Gospel: *And I will ask the Father, and he will give you another advocate to be with you forever. This is the Spirit of truth....*"(14:17) and "*I have said these things to you while I am still with you, but the Advocate, the Holy Spirit, whom the Father will send in my name, will teach you everything and remind you of all that I have said to you.*"(14:25-26)

The emphasis is on the Spirit enlightening their minds as to the truths of Jesus' teachings but without compromising that precious created gift of freedom. How that is done we do not know, and do not need to know. What was important to them was that their freedom to decide what to do and teach was assisted by the Holy Spirit to make the right decisions in the light of those truths. Somehow they become attracted to and convinced by the light of those truths. Today, men (at present) are appointed to positions of office in the Church. Are all these appointments the work of the Holy Spirit or are some merely the work of those who equate such ministry with that of a ruling executive? The history of the Church shows that if those who were appointed to be ministers and leaders subsequently placed more emphasis on power and control than on teaching,

---

53 Decree on the Apostolate of Lay People "Apostolicam Actuositatem" 23.

'feeding' and caring for the followers of Christ, their authority diminished in the eyes of the people of God. At the same time, if there was any kind of control or compulsion, the people's freedom to worship in spirit and truth was denied and they merely surrendered that freedom to another.

Freedom to 'sense' the truth?

It is the authority of the truths of the Gospel which sets us free from those influences which prevent us from growing in love and truth: *"If you continue in my word, you are truly my disciples; and you will know the truth, and the truth will make you free.* (John 8:31-32) Recently, in 2014, there were two events which at first did not seem to be connected. The first was the preparation for and the taking place of the first session of the Synod of Bishops on family life and the second was the publication of the document "Sensus Fidei in the Life of the Church" by the International Theological Commission. However, after studying that document it became clear to me that in fact the two are intimately connected and related to this question of authority.

There is much to applaud in this document in which the Commission has made a serious attempt to express, in not quite plain language but certainly an improvement on other official documents, the theological basis for a better understanding of the concept 'the sense of the faith' which is commonly used in its Latin form 'sensus fidei'. My attention was drawn to the proactive nature of this 'sense' which contains the idea that it motivates the possessor to express it and to put it into practice. It was making sense of the controversy regarding consultation, or rather the lack of it, in not only the preparation of the Synod but also in the actual event. One of the consequences of the very existence of such a 'sense of the faith' is it obliges those in the various offices of the Church to respond by creating spaces for its expression.

Is there such a 'sense', that is, an innate sense of the Christian faith in disciples of Jesus Christ, or are we simply passive receivers of doctrine from those in authority? If there is, does it challenge that authority or does it accept or not accept that authority's teaching? The Theological Commission defines this 'sense' as where *"the faithful have an instinct for the truth of the Gospel, which enables them to recognise and endorse authentic Christian doctrine and practice, and to reject what is false."*[54] That is some statement! It would be hard to find another official statement having such an import as this on any kind of authoritarian tendency in the Church. This is a direct challenge to those office-holders who believe that the 'faithful' are to accept a teaching simply because of their authority of office.

It seems that because of our free appropriation and practice of the teachings and values of the Gospel, with the help of the indwelling of the Holy Spirit, we can act and judge wisely in their application: *"...the sensus fidei, which, as well as enabling a certain discernment with regards to the things of faith, fosters true wisdom and gives rise to proclamation of the truth."*[55] This is not some sudden gift from a sacramental rite but is formed by the living-out of those Gospel values in everyday life. This means that we judge and act almost instinctively with Christian wisdom when we are required to respond to any given situation or idea, but always in the context of our human failings. In other words this 'sense' does not come automatically with our reception of those Gospel values, nor from any particular sacramental rite, but develops in our application of them in the world in which we live. There is a similarity here with the

---

54   International Theological Commission "Sensus Fidei in the Life of the Church", 2.
55   Ibid.(2)

well-known idea of 'common sense', once described to me as 'the almost instinctive ability to make a balanced judgement', except that in the case of the 'sense of the faith' there is the important added dimension of the assistance of the 'Spirit of truth'. (See John 14)

However, this idea of such an individual 'sense of the faith' has always been approached by ordained pastors and office holders in the Church with a high degree of wariness and ambivalence in encouraging its expression. This is largely due to the fear that acceptance of its importance would undermine their perceived 'authority', both in teaching the Gospel truths and values and in governing and ruling 'the faithful'. Once such authority as the latter is believed and taught by those in office, then any idea that the individual Christian has the freedom to express and proclaim their sense of what is being taught challenges such authoritarian attitudes and structures within the Church. If, on the other hand, we accept that the only 'authority' given to the Apostles and therefore the leaders and pastors of today is to preach (teach) the Gospel, make disciples of Christ, baptize them in the name of the Father, Son and Holy spirit,[56] feed, tend and care for them[57], then there is complete harmony between that kind of authority and the 'sense of the faithful'.

A 'sense' or merely sensible?

If we accept that there is such a 'sense', it is also obvious from our own experience and from any sensible appraisal of its existence that also there has to be a judgement as to whether a particular proclamation by a believer, or by sense of the

---

56 Matthew 28:19-20.
57 John 21:15-17.

faithful as a whole ('sensus fidelium'), is merely an opinion with no basis in the Gospel teachings. There has to be a balance between the opinions expressed and an external judgement, otherwise any opinion claimed as authentic 'sense of the faith' may not be of the Gospel of Jesus Christ. This is where the kind of authority given to our leaders, to guide and protect by constantly preaching the truths of the Gospel, by interpreting them in relation to a changing world, leading others to be freely attracted (or not) by those teachings, is one of true leadership. In this way the 'sense of the faithful' is guided, protected and allowed to develop rather than either ignored or crushed under the weight of an authoritarian regime.

The imperative for dialogue and consultation

Are our church leaders obliged to seek out this 'sense', particularly before discussing a topic and making decisions which affect not only every member of the Church but more importantly its mission to the world? The Theological Commission's document states very clearly in refreshing forthright language that there is an obligation placed on those in authority to consult the faithful: *"...accordingly, the faithful and specifically the lay people, should be treated by the Church's pastors with respect and consideration, and consulted in the appropriate way for the good of the Church."* [58] It makes it clear that this is not merely an exercise in public relations but genuine consultation: *"The word 'consult' includes the idea of seeking a judgement or advice as well as enquiring into a matter of fact."* [59]

---

58   Ibid. 120.
59   Ibid.121.

The lack of this kind of positive consultation has often resulted in the non-reception by many of the faithful of the doctrinal and ministerial positions taken by office-holders. This may be the result of an immature sense of the faith of individual believers or indifference of those office-holders to the views of other members of the people of God: *"But in some cases it may indicate that certain decisions have been taken by those in authority without due consideration of the experience and the sensus fidei of the faithful, or without sufficient consultation of the faithful by the magisterium."*[60] This point can clearly be seen in the process arranged for the latest Rome Synod of Bishops on family life held in 2014-15, both in the preparation and the discussions. It proved to the majority of the faithful that there is no permanent system or structure in place whereby the 'sense of the faithful' is part of the consultation and decision-making.

The imperative for 'synodality' in the Church

What kind of change can be made to enable and encourage a true and effective consultation to take place? What I am proposing is not new to the universal Church but in the Roman Catholic wing it has been allowed to 'wither on the vine'. Synodality, with its root meaning of being 'together on the road or journey' or the 'common way', is based on the biblical teaching on communion and fellowship (Gk. koinonia) which always has been at the heart of the life of the Church. However, history shows that the practice of synodality, as the best way for the 'sense of the faith' to be heard at all levels, developed under the influence and authority of Rome into what we know to be exclusively synods of bishops.

---

60   Ibid.123.

The Orthodox churches have always retained the wider expression of synodality in their local and national synods, and later in the early part of the 20th century the Anglican Church set up their present system of parish councils, deanery, diocesan and national synods. In the 1968 Lambeth Conference, the tone was set for subsequent synodal structures in the Anglican Communion, and should be the foundational principle for all Christian administrations: *"The Conference recommends that no major issue in the life of the Church should be decided without full participation of the laity in discussion and in decision."* (Resolution 24). In the Roman Catholic Church in England, the attempts to promote synodality have resulted in little progress, with a variety of forms of parish and diocesan consultative bodies which in practice do not give space for consensus decision-making but more often than not are submissive to an authoritarian bishop or parish priest. National and diocesan synods have been virtually non-existent, yet, in other parts of the world some progress has been made even though tight control has been exercised by bishops and Vatican officials.[61]

The practice of synodality does not mean promoting a political system of democracy in the administration of church life. The need for democratic elements arises from the need for genuine dialogue and subsequent dialogical structures.[62] Such democratic elements breathe new life into the Church, the life of communion with each other in the freedom of the Holy Spirit. Freedom to love God in loving one another has to be protected and nurtured by practices and structures of communion and fellowship (koinonia) in which the 'sense of the faithful'

---

61 In USA, 42 diocesan synods took place between 1983 and 2003: Bradford Hinze "Practices of Dialogue in the Catholic Church"p.63.2006.
62 Ludwig Kaufmann SJ. "Synods of Bishops: Neither 'Concilium' nor 'Synods'" 1990, p.179.

becomes engaged and activated in collective discernment and decision-making in the life of the Church.

Synodality is the key to ensure that the Gospel teaching on authority cannot be corrupted by those who hold an authoritarian viewpoint. Where structures are put in place to ensure full dialogue and consultation at all levels of the Church before decisions are made which affect everyone, the 'sense of the faithful' is given the room to express itself. In fact, the Vatican II document on the Church explicitly states that the 'laity' have the right and the obligation to give their opinion on those things which pertain to the Church, and what is more, institutions should be established for that purpose.[63] In this case, office-holders will have as much effective authority as is conceded to them freely by believers through their faith.[64] This, in turn, provides a check on any kind of authoritarian tendency among office-holders. But where are these institutions or structures to enable and facilitate the so called 'laity' to express their opinion, their sense of the faith? Since Vatican II, any movement to set up such structures has been consistently rejected by office-holders to the extent that even the attempt by Pope Francis in 2014 to consult the 'faithful' in preparation for the Synod on Family Life was a failure because of the lack of such permanent structures.

Once authority in the Church is seen as power to control and impose rather than authority to persuade,[65] the result is inevitably one in which the Gospel message is corrupted in order for such power to be justified. In discussions and documents, appeals and references are made to biblical texts and traditional teachings to provide support for office-holders to govern and

---

63 Dogmatic Constitution on the Church "Lumen Gentium" 37. Vatican Council II. ed Austin Flannery.
64 Karl Rahner SJ. "The Shape of the Church to Come" p.58, 1972.
65 Cf. David S. Cunningham "These Three Are One" 1998, 318-335.

rule the 'faithful' who, as passive subjects surrender their freedom to 'worship in spirit and truth'.

Binding and loosing

A prime example of such control is the constant reference in official church teaching to the text in Matthew's gospel about 'binding and loosing'. It is familiar to all Catholics because it is often quoted in discussions and documents, referred to in homilies at Mass and taught in seminaries, to justify the kind of authority exercised by office-holders in the Church which is often that of power and control. However, when the original Greek is studied the text may have a completely different meaning. The following is the translation given in the normal readings of ch.16:18-19 relating to Jesus' commission to Peter:[66]

"I will give you the keys of the kingdom of heaven, and whatever you bind on earth <u>will be bound</u> in heaven, and whatever you loose on earth <u>will be loosed</u> in heaven." (my underlining)

The official teaching of the Church authorities is that this gives Peter, and by logical deduction those succeeding him in that commission, the authority to make decisions which are then given the authority of God in heaven. For example, this has been used in the traditional teaching and practice of 'excommunication' whereby the Pope has the power to prevent a particular person from receiving the sacraments, and even from entering the kingdom of heaven! This interpretation can be seen clearly in the 'Catechism of the Catholic Church' published in 1994, *"The words bind and loose mean: whomever you exclude from your communion will be excluded from communion with*

---

66   E.g. New Revised Version, New Jerusalem Bible, New International Version, King James Version.

God; whomever you receive anew into your communion, God will welcome back into his. " [67] This is symptomatic of that kind of authoritarianism which is diametrically opposed to the truth which sets you free. Even more significant is the mentality behind the statement that pastors and office-holders have the authority and power to exclude people from communion with God, the direct relationship made freely available through the death and resurrection of his Son. The last thing I want to do is descend into some kind of technical argument over particular nuances of translation, but because of the importance placed on this text by church authorities for their understanding of this power over the lives of others, a look at what may be the correct context for this text is required if we are to get near to its true meaning.

"Your will be done"

The background imagery here is that of the kingdom of heaven as a city with gates through which we have to pass through in order to eventually attain the life of that city. Heaven is therefore imagined in spatial terms to convey that idea of a journey towards and entry into God's promised new life. The next image is that of the 'keys' to the gates of that city in order to show that entry can only be obtained by means of those 'keys'. Jesus gives these 'keys' to Peter and the other apostles, but this does not mean that they have been given the role of controlling who enters Heaven. Peter and the apostles are not being set-up as ecclesiastical power figures on whose personal decisions hang people's fates.[68] It means that the authoritative

---

67   Catechism of the Catholic Church, 1443-1445, published by Geoffrey Chapman,1994.

68   John Nolland "The New International Greek Testament Commentary:The Gospel of Matthew" 2005, p.677.

truths of the Gospel are the 'keys' which are given to Peter and his successors to possess, safeguard, and to teach in order for others to enter the new life God has prepared for them (heaven). If Peter and the apostles, and subsequent leaders, continue to use those 'keys' then their teachings and judgements will continue to be endorsed in heaven. It is these truths which are the 'keys' to unlock the way to that new life in Heaven, and it is all leaders and teachers who are to show that the most important key to that life is Jesus himself.[69]

The 'binding and loosing' text continues within the context of the imagery of entering or not being able to enter Heaven. Much of this imagery is in the Old Testament context, particularly in the ideas concerning the battle between good and evil, where, for instance, evil spirits bind people to certain conditions and behaviour. We are familiar with the stories in the New Testament where such persons are 'loosed' from an illness or condition which is believed to be a 'binding' to an evil spirit. A good example is in Luke 13:16 where a crippled woman is healed by Jesus through the imagery of being 'loosed' from such a binding. However, all such healings, all such 'loosings' are put in the context of the direction of the future lives of the persons involved. In using the terminology of binding and loosing for the kind of authority given by Jesus to Peter and the apostles, Matthew is drawing upon that same imagery where people are freed from whatever binds them to a particular way of life by the direction of travel which they need to take in order to follow Jesus as the way, truth and the life. Peter and the apostles' possession of the 'keys' primarily involves them pointing to Jesus in all that they do and teach in order that they are able to make judgements as to what binds people to a sinful life and what frees them for a life in Heaven.

---

69 Nolland, p.677.

Whatever Peter and the apostles and their successors decide in their role as pastors of God's people, it will be in conformity to the will of God, as it is in heaven, *if it is true to the Gospel*. The earthly actions of Peter and the Apostles (see also 18:18) follow the heavenly actions. It is a promise not of divine endorsement, but of divine guidance to empower Peter, the apostles and their successors to decide in accordance with what God has already determined. [70]

The text, like all the others, has to be interpreted in the light of the whole of the particular gospel. Whatever the life is in heaven, and we cannot know until we get there what that means, there is complete union with God himself. This theme of doing everything on earth according to the will of God, as revealed in and by his Son, is also in the 'Our Father' prayer taught by Jesus, *"Your will be done on earth as it is in heaven"*. To say that the first text implies that God will always back whatever the leaders of the Church decide for his people, right or wrong, is the opposite of the meaning of that text and the prayer taught by Jesus. It cannot mean, in the light of the whole gospel, that the future leaders in the Church will always be right, their teaching infallible. The history of the Church has shown the falseness of such an interpretation in the many errors of its leaders, both in doctrine and morals. It is only in their adherence to the truths, the 'keys', of the Gospel that they can be confident of being in union with the will of God in heaven.

What do the scripture scholars say about this text? I do not want to get into the game of pitting one expert against another for that would get me nowhere in searching for an answer, as there are many differences of opinion. There is certainly no agreement as to the literal meaning, with scholars arguing for and against the traditional interpretation. However, there can be consensus as to the meaning when it is interpreted in the

---

70   R.T.France "Commentary on Matthew" p.454 & 627.

context of the gospel as a whole. The proposal *"that in order to be true, an interpretation or a new meaning of a biblical text must correspond to the basic line of Jesus' story."*[71] is generally held to be the only way to reach an understanding of a text in which the original Greek grammar can suggest different interpretations. At the same time, it is generally agreed that there can be no reading back into the meaning of the text any teaching which arises from today's existing doctrines and practices in the Church. Jesus did not lay down a blueprint for how his followers, leaders and pastors should develop the doctrines, forms and structures of the Church, but instead laid its foundation on the truths revealed by its founder and saviour. If, subsequently, all teaching and practice retains that vital connection to those foundational truths, the dangers of scriptural fundamentalism and surface-reading of texts[72] can be avoided.

Authority in 'office'

The above example is illustrative of how the authority of 'office' can lead to distortion of the very message its holder is supposed to teach and protect. There are different kinds of authority in the societies in which we live, and each has a particular source and function. As a police officer, like the centurion in the New Testament, I had the authority to tell others "do this, do that". Such authority was given to me by a higher authority of the Crown and Parliament to keep 'The Peace', to protect the country's citizens, to prevent and detect crime, and many other duties. The acceptance by society of such a power is based on the recognition that it is necessary for the common good

---

71   Ulrich Luz "Studies in Matthew" p.3 & 179.
72   James D.G.Dunn "The Partings of the Ways" 2006, p.xxxi.

in a democratic society. Without it, the weak would be at the mercy of the strong, the good at the mercy of the bad, and the well-being of society suffer from its enemies. That is the nature of that particular office, but *how* such an authority is put into practice is of vital importance for that well-being of society. If it is misunderstood or abused by its holders the acceptance of the office itself is liable to be undermined.

There is, also, the authority of office in management and administration of organisations and commercial companies, as well as in government departments. This kind of authority is necessary for the implementation of policies and the fulfilment of the goals set by leaders and managers. Are such similar powers of authority necessary and desirable for the Church?

Policing the Church?

First, I will take the question of whether a type of 'policing' authority is required in the institutional and administrative aspects. Should there be any kind of compulsion, with its corresponding consequences of enforcement by sanctions or punishments, in order to protect the members of the Church? If so, from what are they being protected, and who should have the authority to enforce that protection?

When I tried to address these questions it became clear that I needed to identify the nature and purpose of the Church as an institution. To answer this fully would be to embark on a comprehensive work comparable to the great historical works already in existence. However, what we have in the teachings of the Gospel are the essential principles and values with which we can identify the foundations upon which the body of the Church grows. From the Gospel we see that the three most important things are faith, hope and love. These should be the hallmarks of the Church in everything it does; without them there is no

Church. Should there be some kind of authority in place which exercises control and supervision over the everyday life of the body's members in order to nurture their faith, hope and love? Is the office of the Pope, the various clerical departmental offices, the diocesan bishops and priests, the various ordinances of Canon Law, meant to be that controlling authority? Clearly not according to the purposes of their roles within the body of the Church, to serve the building-up of that body in faith, hope and love by teaching and preaching the Gospel, making disciples of all nations and baptizing them in the name of the Father and of the Son and of the Holy Spirit. (Matt.28:19)

Somehow, over the first two millennia, that authority, that commission to the apostles and their successors, was changed by those who developed a different kind of authoritative power in addition to that given by Christ. How that happened is part of the study of the history of the Church, but the fact is that today we have an institution which has developed its own methods and laws to control what its members can do or not do. It is no wonder then that in order for such control to be effective there developed methods of enforcement which in the past led to heinous crimes against individuals and groups, such as 'burning at the stake', beheadings, torture, imprisonment, banishments and excommunications .

Today, that enforcement has become more 'civilised' through various methods, but with the punishments of excommunication, of silencing those who dare to voice criticism, are still part of that armoury of sanctions. Unfortunately, the view that the leaders and office-holders of the Church have a commission to rule and govern the people of God still pervades the thinking and decision-making of those responsible for administering the life of the Church.

What about the question of authority in management and administration? Is the nature of the Church meant to be such that a system of checks and balances, of rules and regulations, of managers and supervisors, is necessary for it to carry out its commission from Christ? It is certainly true that if the present structures of the Church as a visible organisation are to function, it has to have rules which guide and facilitate its activities. Once it is said that a 'movement' for a particular belief and way of life requires rules and laws to direct and control its activities and progress, then the question arises of whether that requires a comprehensive system of management and supervision, with corresponding arrangements for enforcement.

The question which intrigues me is whether the development of the Church, as a very structured, managed, supervised and controlled organisation as we know it today, gave birth to the development of the theology behind the practices of worship, priesthood and authority, or whether the opposite is true that for such practices to survive and develop as they have done they developed out of a theology which failed to keep its roots in the Gospel? I suggest that both have been factors in the development of the forms and structures which enclose and protect a theology justifying authoritarian control of the Church, yet the one factor which underlies both is that failure to maintain that essential focus on its roots and nourishment in Jesus Christ and his Gospel.

Protecting the Church

Christ's commission to Peter and the other apostles, to care for and 'feed' his Church, to preach his Gospel, the 'good news', to baptize and teach, subsequently meant that they and their activities soon met with opposition, often violent and fatal. The history of the Church has shown that this has continued up to the present day. Does the Church, in particular its mission and its message, need protecting? If so, what form should this take and who should do it? This is where that enigmatic statement of Jesus, *"Give (render) therefore to the emperor the things that are the emperor's, and to God the things that are God's"*, [73] can help to understand the relationship between civic duties and duty to God. In the context of any needed protection, the duty to protect the well-being of citizens, whatever their particular beliefs and religious practices, lies with the elected civic authorities. The kind of protection needed by members of the Church in addition to that is the protection of the truth of the Gospel by those elected to be its preachers and teachers. Our freedom to live according to our belief in the society in which we live can only be protected by the civic authorities whom the citizens have given their mandate to govern and protect that society. That kind of authority to govern is not given to individuals or institutions of the Christian Church, where its members give their allegiance to a completely different kind of authority, that of the truth about God, about mankind and its future, as revealed in and through his Son. These two kinds of authority are the two sides of the same 'coin'; they are the reality of the one life of the citizen, allegiance to God and to the State.

Leaders or bosses?

If we believe that the nature of the Church is such that in order for it to be able to carry-out its mission of bringing the Gospel of Jesus Christ to all peoples and all generations it needs structures, offices, supervisors (overseers?), managers and controllers, then, of course, it takes on the character of a large commercial company. It has a 'product' to sell, i.e. the Gospel, not one it has manufactured, but one it has been given to pass on to others. This work of 'distribution' requires

---

73   Matt.22:21; Mk.12:17; Lk.20:25.

workers, managers and bosses on a world-wide scale, with corresponding administration structures, rules and regulations with appropriate enforcement procedures to ensure an efficient operation. Such a global corporation would have tremendous marketing power which, if not tempered with checks and balances as to how such power is used, would be able to control the supply and quality of its product without any fear of competition. It would have the same power as a totalitarian state in which, because there is only one undemocratic authority, there is total control of the lives of its people. Protection and enforcement is paramount in preserving the status quo. Such 'globalization' in commerce has its dangers, as civic leaders and social scientists are now realising. The negative effects on societies can be seen in the power of these huge corporations to control markets to such an extent that also they can have a significant influence on individual governmental institutions. Where such power resides in a decreasing amount of 'hands', history shows it inevitably leads to either personal corruption of leaders and officials or to extreme measures to maintain its position.

The Church, in the form that we see the institution today, is no exception to this danger of assuming great power over its people. If, on the other hand, we believe that the nature of the Church is such that its mission is one of presenting the truth of the Gospel to all peoples so that in their God-given freedom they are led and persuaded to be attracted to the truths arising from that revelation, then the kind of organisation needed for facilitating that work is of a completely different type. Common sense tells us that for such work to take place there has to be some kind organisation with suitable persons as leaders, teachers, preachers as well as those with skills and experience of supervision and management. In such an organisation, what kind of leadership is required for the work of its mission? Does such leadership require the kind of authority exercised by the boss of a commercial or political global corporation, or is there something in that role which is inimical to the mission of the Church?[74]

Form at the service of mission

In answering these questions it is essential to go to the foundational roots of any movement or initiative in order to identify the motivation for its particular form and practices, and to apply them to the present day. It was precisely in this context that Pope John identified the purpose of the Council of Vatican II which he set in motion in 1959 in a two-fold approach of updating and returning to the sources of the Christian faith, with its central focus of *'The centrality of Christ'* for its mission to the world. This is the test for any formal structure in the Church; does its form serve its mission? If its form is such that it perpetuates the practice of authority as control and compulsion, thus depriving members' freedom to worship in spirit and truth, then that form no longer preserves that focus of the centrality of Christ and his gospel. What has become central is the authority of office, as in the dictum of a father to a young child, "do what I say", with the added threat "or else" as a consequence of disobedience. This infantilisation of the laity has become a subject much discussed in the present day,[75] and is indicative of a growing resistance at the grass roots to the continuation of authoritarianism in the various offices of the Church.

What is clear is that the New Testament does not give leaders of the Church the kind of dominative or jurisdictional

---

74   cf. Pope Francis "Evangelii Gaudium" (The Joy of the Gospel), 95.
75   E.g. Paul Lakeland "The Liberation of the Laity" 2004, p.211; John L. McKenzie "The Tension Between Authority and Freedom" in "Readings In Church Authority" Gerard Mannion et al., p.125.

power which exists in secular societies.[76] Rather it shows the need for pastors, not priests, whose mandate from Christ is to 'feed' and care for his people, even if there is a necessity for administrative systems where there have to be managers and overseers. What is important is that whatever system of management is employed it has to be at the service of the people and their pastors, not the other way around.

This is equally true of the relationship between the pastor and the members of the local Church if it is to serve their freedom to worship 'in spirit and truth'. Christ did not set us free from the slavery of sin in order for us to become slaves of a new order of rules and laws: *"For freedom Christ has set us free. Stand firm, therefore, and do not be subject again to a yoke of slavery."* (Galatians 5:1). The apostle Paul was referring to the problem of those early Christians who were being persuaded that they needed to submit to the requirements of the old law, whereas Paul was showing them that it is not submission to all the rules and regulations that Christ wants but *"faith operating effectively through love."* (5:6). The image of God which such subjection portrays has been described as a "bookkeeping God of legalism"[77], and not that revealed by Christ. Paul's example of authority was not a building-up of a sacral relationship of spiritual control and subordination, and in fact he was totally set against such a possibility.[78]

In 2012, on the occasion of the fiftieth anniversary of the Second Vatican Council, a group of 104 international Catholic scholars signed a "Jubilee Declaration" in which it highlighted seven reforms needed in the Catholic Church. To my mind, the final statement is a useful summary of what I have tried to say

---

76   John L. McKenzie "The Tension Between Authority and Freedom" in "Readings in Church Authority" Gerard Mannion et al., p.121.

77   E.de W.Burton "The Epistle to the Galatians" 277 quoted in James D.G.Dunn "The Epistle to the Galatians" 266.

78   James D. G. Dunn "The Epistle to the Galatians" 1975, p.278.

in more detail about the kind of authority in the Church which draws its justification from the Gospel of Jesus Christ:

"The exercise of authority in our Church should emulate the standards of openness, accountability and democracy achieved in modern society. Leadership should be seen to be honest and credible; inspired by humility and service; breathing concern for people rather than preoccupation with rules and discipline; radiating a Christ who makes us free; and listening to Christ's Spirit who speaks and acts through each and every person."[79]

---

79 www.churchauthority.org/index.asp

A Church fit for purpose?

If what I have written above about 'authority' in the Church is true, how would the Church function according to its purpose? Given the reality that we have a Church which is ruled and governed by office-holders who have been taught and trained to believe that they have been given such authority through a sacred ordination in which the Holy Spirit is invoked to empower and sanction such a commission, what would the Church look like and function if it was true to its roots? Where do we find these roots?

Members of the Catholic Church have become accustomed to being told that these roots can be found in the dual resources of the Bible and Tradition but with the added teaching that they contain the 'sacred deposit' of the faith which is entrusted to the whole of the Church.[80] The roots of that 'sacred deposit' is the Gospel of Jesus Christ as revealed in him and by him to his followers with assistance of his Holy Spirit. These roots give life and nourishment to the Church – he is the vine, we the branches to bear the fruit (John 15). Anything which cuts us off, separates us from this source, is not rooted in the person of Jesus Christ as 'the way, truth and life.'

---

80 Catechism 84.

In the history of the Church we have seen many branches and much fruit, but at the same time many errors of teaching, conduct and practices which did not have their roots in the person and word of the Son of God. Despite the witness of the first disciples and their leaders and the witness of the 'fathers' of the Church during the first three centuries, there was always the danger of the 'weeds' attempting to choke the 'wheat' growing together in the same soil.[81] This situation has continued up to the present time, with the Church having gone through many times where it seemed the 'weeds' would overcome the 'wheat' but for those leaders and true witnesses who retained that vital connection with the very source of life and truth. As far back as 1972, the influential theologian, Karl Rahner, was asking the question as to where and how the Church in its actual life and action was, and still is, itself the cause of the decline of an explicitly ecclesial Christianity. The question he proposed, *"was this the result of an old-fashioned theology and proclamation, of a life-style on the part of office-holders and other Christians which makes Christianity look historically obsolete, and so on?"*[82] has still to be fully answered.

Communicating God's truth and love

Before we can consider whether the Church is 'fit for purpose', that is, whether it is in fact carrying out its mission from Christ in a way which that purpose can be realised, it makes sense to identify what is that purpose. The Vatican II document on the Church 'Lumen gentium' (lit. 'light of the gentiles') puts it very succinctly: *"The one mediator, Christ, established and ever sustains here on earth his holy Church, the community of faith,*

---

81 Matthew 13.
82 "The Shape of the Church to Come" p.31.

hope and charity, as a visible organization through which he communicates truth and grace to all men."(8) [83] Setting aside the non-inclusive language of 'men' and the traditional usage of the term 'grace' which tends to impersonalise that loving action of God which the original Greek term 'charis' denotes, nevertheless the statement is a good one to use as a means for discussion as to whether the existing forms and structures of the Church are suitable for its mission and purpose. Has the Church lost that focus of communicating the truth and loving actions of God in his Son, Jesus Christ, through their Holy Spirit, because of the adoption of teachings, structures and practices which tend to obscure or distort that purpose?

If certain teachings and practices of the Church have lost their vital connection to those 'roots' and the purpose of the Church, what can be done about it? If the forms of our worship, priesthood and authority have lost much of that vital connection to the central teachings of the Gospel of Jesus Christ, what changes should take place to restore that relationship? Throughout the history of the Church there have been many individuals who have tried to keep the Church focussed on the essential truths of the Gospel, but they were up against those leaders and office-holders who allowed themselves to be influenced by other ideas of what Christ's Church should be in its nature and practices. Erroneous ideas, as I have outlined above, relating to authority, priesthood and worship, led to the kind of Church we see today, where its official image of God has strayed from that revealed by his Son. As a consequence, at different times, much of the leadership in the Church developed along parallel lines with that of civic rulers whose office depended upon absolute control of subjects and practices.

---

83 "Vatican Council II. The Conciliar and Post Conciliar Documents" ed. Austin Flannery, O.P. 1992.

What forms should leadership in the Church take to reflect the teachings of Jesus Christ about its life and purpose?

The question of gender in leadership

This subject is of major importance for the future of a Church which should be reflecting the full image of God as revealed by his Son and their Spirit. There is no biblical or theological justification for the position of leadership in the Church, whether held in the position of 'Pope', bishop or pastor, to be held exclusively by a man. The arguments put forward by those who teach the opposite position are unconvincing because they are based on (i) an illogical deduction from the social conditions at the time of the biblical texts being written, and (ii) a kind of fundamentalism in which there is reliance on a tradition where, because something decided by men has always been the case it must be right, especially if subsequent revered leaders have followed that tradition. To say that because Jesus chose men to be his first disciples, his first leaders, then subsequent leaders have no right to be other than of the male gender, is an example of a fundamentalist view of biblical history where there is no differentiation between the central teachings and those secondary details which are only relevant to the times and place. If we follow this principle, then the fact that Jesus chose Jews and not Gentiles to be his first apostles would mean that all subsequent leaders and pastors would have to be Jews![84]

---

84   Karen Armstrong "The End of Silence" (1993), p.46.

An incomplete ministry

This error is compounded by the adoption of the practice and theology of the 'ordained priesthood' where pastors become priests offering Christ's sacrifice at altars (see above). Once it is said that the priest at the altar is acting in the person of Christ as an 'alter Christus' (other Christ) then it is a small step to teach that because Christ is a man then anyone acting as Christ has to be a man. If we set aside for the moment the question of whether the office and cult of the ordained 'priest' should exist at all, even the existing teaching and practices surrounding the reservation of such an office to men only serves to reinforce a distorted image of God. If leaders and ministers are to reflect that image in their care and 'feeding' the people of God, being men is only half that image, for it is male and female who become one in Christ[85] who in himself reveals that reality (glory) of God.[86]

Although the social conditions of women have changed considerably compared to those at the time of the early Church, the position and status of women in ministry has changed far more slowly than it has outside the Church. The reasons for this are varied and have been discussed at length but the underlying error perpetuated by the leaders and office-holders throughout the history of the Church has been that which equated its ministry to that exercised only by a priestly brotherhood. This may not have excluded women as such but when that priestly caste took on the character of not only the Old Testament male priesthood of offering sacrifices on behalf of the people but also certain characteristics of the Roman Empire's pagan worship, for example male priestly sacrifice at altars and male Roman rituals and vestments, it prevented the inclusion of

---

85   Paul "Letter to the Galatians" 3:27-28.
86   "Letter to the Hebrews" 1:3.

women. Once such a clerical caste became firmly in control of the leadership and worship in the life of the Church the role of women became one of subordination to that of men.

Tradition for tradition's sake

To use the argument that the 'tradition' of the Church has always been one in which only men are chosen for this role of ordained priests is to resort not to reasons which justify this position but to a 'traditionalism' which Jesus himself criticized in the attitudes of the Pharisees and scribes, *"Why do you break the commandment of God for the sake of your tradition?.....So, for the sake of your tradition, you make void the word of God.* [87] What is more, Matthew has Jesus quoting a relevant verse from Isaiah, *"This people honour me with their lips, but their hearts are far from me; in vain do they worship me, teaching human precepts as doctrines."* (29:13).

The 'Tradition' of the Church is the handing-on of the central truths of the Christian faith and the handing-over by God of his Spirit for us to live-out our lives 'in spirit and truth' as the people of God. Any attempt to bind people to a particular time and place in the past, to particular social conditions and practices of that time and place, to particular forms of worship and ministry of a bygone age, is, first of all, a denial of the immanence of the trinitarian God, and second, a denial of the need for us to 'move on' [88] in seeking new ways of 'giving ourselves' to God (worshipping) in the here and now of time. It is only then that we are able to be disciples of Jesus Christ in carrying out his mission to others. It is only then that the 'handing-on', the Christian 'Tradition', is not obscured by that

---

87 Matthew 15:3-7; cf. Mark 7:6-8.
88 Cf. Letter to the Hebrews ch.5.

'fossilized traditionalism' [89] which binds the living word of God to a past age.

For the sake of Christ's mission, we need both women and men in ministry in all parts of the Church if we are to reflect the right image of God in whom male and female exist as one. Therefore, to teach that women are not suitable to be 'ordained priests' because the Church has no authority to change what Jesus did when he chose only men to be his apostles and disciples,[90] (setting aside the argument against priests per se), amounts to a type of blindness to what was really important to Jesus, that is, choosing messengers (apostles) who would be acceptable to the people *at that time.* This was a pragmatic decision and therefore he did not make it as something to be followed for all time.

The right people for the right job

All Catholics have grown up with the experience of roles of leadership in all areas of the Church being reserved for clerics of some kind or other, the consequences of which has been the enormous growth in the phenomenon of 'clericalism', a policy of upholding the power of the clergy. Whatever aspect of the Church's life we can identify, the control and influence that is exerted at all levels by this male clerical brotherhood is absolute. Even in the case of the female religious orders, the final word is possessed by male clerics, either in the form of diocesan bishops or those wielding power in the Vatican 'headquarters'. Even if the notion of a priestly caste for acts of worship is accepted, the idea that all the organisational and administrative structures of

---

89   "A Fearful Symmetry? The Complementarity of Men and Women in Ministry."
     A.M Allchin, et al, 1992.
90   "Catechism of the Catholic Church", 1577.

the Church should be led and controlled by that same priestly brotherhood is a false understanding of the reality of Christian ministry and is indicative of that desire for control.

The existence of this all-pervading clericalism in the Church, particularly in relation to leadership and ministry, means that even in matters of organisation and administration there has to be a cleric in one of the forms of priest, bishop, archbishop, cardinal, in charge of everyday affairs. The idea that in order to run a particular department, whether a parish, diocese, or Vatican congregation, a 'lay' person is unsuited to do this because he/she has not gone through a ritual of 'sacerdotal ordination' and therefore quite incapable of holding a ministerial office, is indicative of how far the original error of re-introducing a priestly caste has influenced the understanding of Christian ministry. The history of the Church shows that despite being steeped in the many facets of clerical life, many priests, at all levels of the Church, were unsuitable to hold ministerial office. Being 'sacramentally ordained' was no defence against false doctrine and moral corruption, even though the development of a mystique of holiness in priests led people to believe it did.

The development of lay missionaries, particularly in the reformed churches, shows that if there is no bar to suitable persons, male or female, of choosing a life dedicated to bringing the Good News to others, the right people can be found for the different tasks of Christ's mission to the world. The task of bringing the teachings of the Gospel, of bringing others to 'worship' God in spirit and truth, is not dependent on being a member of a priestly caste. This separation of 'priest and lay' became the norm only since the 12th and 13th centuries when the teaching on priestly ordination as a sacrament became official, e.g. General Council of Lyons in 1274. Such teaching included the notion of the ordination leaving an indelible 'mark' on the priest which even persisted after death! From then on, the separation of lay and priest became much more a fact of life in the Church, with the priest having control of what the lay person should think and do. The consequences of this division of the 'laos', the whole people of God, into clerical and lay, has been felt throughout the Christian Church to such an extent that 'ministry' became almost fully associated with the ordained priesthood.

Ministry as a 'charism', not a sacerdotal function.

If, as I suggest, the development of clericalism, with its mystique of the priest, is inimical to that taught by Christ and through his apostles, what should 'ministry' look like in a Church true to its roots and able to adapt to new times? Clearly there should be no limitation as to gender of its ministers, nor should it be restricted to a particular caste or brotherhood. No one person or grouping should have a monopoly on serving the Gospel in the communities of the 'People of God'. The different forms of ministry are described in Paul's letters as "charismata",[91] that is, different charisms of the Holy Spirit. We often hear this said, but often only lip-service is paid to this teaching of the NT.

What exactly is a 'charism'? It is often interpreted as a 'gift' but this doesn't quite get to the nub of the Gospel, because if it is left as that without trying to understand its relationship to our own free spirit, it is as though we are impelled by such a gift to act in a certain way, e.g. to seek to be a 'minister'. Unfortunately, such a view of 'charisms' is not uncommon in the history of the Church, and often resulted in ministers regarding themselves as being apart from others, of being in a privileged position, of being closer to God, of having a sacral status.

---

91   1Corinthians 12:4ff.

Charisms are to do with how God's loving action (Gk. charis) enters our lives by the action of his Holy Spirit, not by force but by the union of Spirit to spirit. It is in this way that we are motivated to freely respond to that act of love in whatever way it signifies. This may well be a motivation to serve Our Lord in some form of ministry in his Church, but this does not mean the minister is 'set apart' from the community he/she is to serve. Indeed, such ministry has the very opposite meaning. In order to serve that 'koinonia', that fellowship and communion, which should be the hallmark of any Christian community, its ministers should be in solidarity with each member. This can only be done if that person is one of the members chosen by them for a particular role, not as someone 'outside' through membership of a particular brotherhood which can only be joined by an appointment and ordination process and, moreover, is imposed upon the community by a senior minister such as a bishop. Charisms are given for the building-up of the Church in love and truth, as a community functioning as the body of Christ. The charism of ministry is not given for the building-up of a priestly brotherhood but is to be expressed in many different forms according to the needs of the Church under the inspiration of the Holy Spirit.[92]

From the community, for the community.

What would such a local ministry look like in practice if it is to be in communion with the heart of the Gospel? Clearly, the members of the Church should have good idea of what is required of a minister and the qualities of the person to be chosen. This would mean a completely new approach for understanding 'Christian ministry' through a series of talks

---

92 Paul's letter to Corinthians 1, chs.12-14; Romans 12:3-8.

and discussions at local level under the guidance of elected leaders and advisers. Notice should be taken of the guidance of regional and national leaders (bishops?) and internationally respected theologians. But, and this is a big 'but', for *guidance* only and not for surrender of that God-given freedom. This would then identify the needs of the community which require particular ministers for particular roles, but it would also identify the qualities and type of person needed for pastoral leadership which reflects the heart of the Gospel of Jesus Christ. The important principle is for that person to be *chosen by the local community* to lead them in communal prayer gatherings, preaching, celebration of the Eucharist, etc., or in policy and decision-making team meetings.

What kind of leadership?

It is fruitful to consider what Christian leadership, true to the heart of the Gospel, is not. It is not controlling, dictatorial, authoritarian, and remote. It is not self-serving, ambition promoting, with an eye on rank, position and title. It does not desire obedience for the sake of the leader being obeyed. In the context of those churches which have a system of priestly ordination, it is not a 'priestly' role where the leader takes on the role of mediator. The leader does not become the focus of the community, to the extent that everything is channelled through his person to the detriment of the community's direct relationship with Our Lord. Much emphasis has been placed on the communal aspect of Christian life but this does not mean that it replaces that vital personal access to God of individual believers. Both realities exist together for the building-up of the Church as the 'body of Christ'. You cannot have that Spirit-filled fellowship (koinonia) with one another without first having that personal fellowship with God through his Son. It can be said, and there is an element of truth in this, that, in the context of authoritarianism in the Church, it is easier for office-holders to exercise control over community life than over the personal life of individuals. Whatever is the truth, the reality is that both are necessary for the Christian life to be rooted in Jesus Christ.

Leadership in service

Christian leadership, above all, is one of service to the community, where such service is seen in the leader by not only being wise in advising the community but also in facilitating its communal acts of worship as a service, a 'giving-up' of themselves to God. In this last context, the leader is not there to impose something on the community or control their service but to be their guide and helper. In practice, of course, this means the leader of the communal service, whether it is a Eucharistic celebration or not, is given the duty of leading those prayers and actions which are always those of the gathered community. The leader guides and facilitates their service, the nature and details of which the community expect to be in communion with the heart of the Gospel.

This can be a particular ministry in itself without the need for that person to be responsible for everything else in the local community/parish. The traditional practice for the pastor to have multiple responsibilities of leadership is not only bad for the pastor but also is detrimental to the local mission of the Church. When I look back to the time when there was a parish priest with three or four curates running the parish, the various ministries were shared among them. Today, there is the situation that, because of the dramatic decline in vocations to the sacerdotal priesthood, in many cases a parish community is served by one pastor who is also responsible for another nearby parish. This creates serious stress for that pastor because of his historical role of controlling everything in the life of each parish. In the future, there has to be division of ministerial responsibilities to such an extent that, for example, there is a separate liturgical minister who has no other responsibility, whereas, the 'pastor' of a community should be just that and no more, rather than the present situation where he is often responsible for the whole administration of parish life. The development of lay 'parish managers or administrators', particularly in the U.S.A., has been a positive development in freeing-up the pastor's time and space for his particular ministry. Any corresponding development in the U.K. has been very slow because of the resistance to such relinquishment of control.

No need for a sacerdotal functionary

In the central act of service at the celebration of the Eucharist, the leader will be visible and audible to the congregation but should not assume such a position of visible dominance as to diminish the communal act because of the perceived role of 'priest' dominating the proceedings. Unfortunately, this is what happens in many services where, because of the present ideas and rules on the role of minister/priest, the leader becomes the focus to such an extent that if there is no minister/priest available the community is unable to gather together and celebrate the Eucharist. In the Catholic Church, the minister as 'priest' has become indispensable, and therefore takes away the right of the community to 'worship in spirit and truth' without him. At the time of writing, I read and hear about bishops closing parishes because they have insufficient priests in their dioceses. To say that a local community cannot gather to do what Jesus asked them to do in remembrance of his life, death and resurrection unless an ordained priest presides, and they cannot function as a community serving God and each other without him, is not only bad ecclesiology but also antithetic to the heart of the Gospel. This comes from working out a theology from traditional and ideological practices rather than being developed from the theology of the Gospel. There is absolutely no valid reason why a local (parish) community cannot elect one of their own to lead them in a Eucharistic service in which they are responding to our Lord's invitation at his last Passover. Jesus did not commission his apostles to offer his sacrifice nor a ritual organised and controlled by their successors as priests. Man-made laws such as those relating to who can and cannot be the leader at the Eucharist in the 'Mass' are, by their very nature, part of a system of control and order, with good intentions or otherwise. The New Testament story of Jesus' words and actions at his 'Last Supper' with his disciples cannot be taken as justifying any such rule, let alone the idea of a brotherhood of priests who can be the only ones to "do this in remembrance of me"(Luke 22:19). Indeed, in John's Gospel, which was written at the end of the 1st century, that last Passover meal was also the occasion for Jesus' teaching in his washing the disciples' feet as a symbolic example of loving service for them to follow as an antidote to any ideas of authoritarian control or self-aggrandizment.

A small example of how a leader of a communal service facilitates the act of the gathered community was when I took part in a celebration of the Eucharist at a Catholic Mass at a special occasion. For the first half of the service, the priest led the prayers from *within the body of the community* and only moved to the sanctuary and 'altar' for the blessing and breaking of the bread and preparation of the wine prior to their 'consecration'. This act of solidarity reinforced the meaning of the Eucharist as a communal act rather than the focus being on a leader who dominates the proceedings and who is the only person who can initiate and bring about the presence of the

Risen Christ in the bread and wine *because of his sacerdotal ordination*. Nevertheless, even though the particular priest tried to show that it is the gathered people, including their leader, who are called by Christ to pray and be with him in a particular way, because of his ordained role he could not stand down from his official priestly position and allow them to fulfil their right to 'worship in spirit and truth' with him or without him, if necessary.

Leadership and 'ministering'

The celebration of the Eucharist is the primary act of the community's offering of thanks to God the Father for the gift and 'sacrifice' of his son Jesus Christ, and at the same time is the primary source of the continuing gift of a share in the divine life of the Father, Son and Holy Spirit (cf. John 6:51-63). This sounds fine, but what does it really mean for our everyday lives? Is it something we 'experience' or is it something which requires faith? Certainly the latter, but it is clear from the whole Gospel that what we do outside of those celebrations demonstrates how we live-out that communion in all the different situations of everyday life. The Eucharist 'feeds' and nourishes that life but it is not imposed on us as though we are simply 'plugged-in' to a source like an electrical connection. There is always a reaction to an action, and Jesus' gift of 'life' asks for that reaction to be our free response in faith, hope and love in the way we express them in our lives.

How does this affect the role of pastors in their task of offering leadership and ministry to the members of the Church in the context of that life offered in the Eucharist? The problem is that it is going to be very hard for those leaders and ministers whose training and mindset has been formed by a tradition and ecclesiology which arose and developed from a reluctance to lose pre-Christian and Roman ideas of worship, priesthood and authority, despite, for example, Paul's teachings. How can this be changed so that the light of the Gospel expressed in the mission of the Church is not obscured by such authoritarian and hierarchical control? How can we have ministers of the Gospel who are not practitioners of canon law and mediators of 'grace' through control of the sacramental life of the Church, but who guide and care for those they are called to serve?

Appearance of unity

The fact that there are ministers who, despite the oppressive structures within which they are required to serve the mission of the Church, demonstrate willingness to step outside and serve the freedom of people to worship in spirit and truth, means that there is hope of change. Such ministers are beacons of light in the gloom produced by closed minds and shrouded hearts. However, it is the people of God, who must find their voice and express their sense of the faith ('sensus fidei') and from whom must come the ministers and leaders of tomorrow. What would attract men and women to become true ministers of the Gospel in a Church founded and built on faith, hope and love? Not power, control, status, ambition, wealth, security, but the motivation to lead, guide, encourage, and serve such a church. This would require the long standing arrangement of a pyramidal church structure of a descending hierarchical power of Pope, bishops and clergy to the 'faithful' to be replaced by that of a circular structure of all ministers in communion with each other and with Christ at the centre. This would facilitate that unity which has so often been talked about but which so often has been expressed in terms of preserving the status quo to avoid disputes and schisms rather than unity in the truth of the Gospel which can only be expressed in the diversity of time, place and culture. There can be no place for that false unity of appearance which subordinates truth to a "cosy traditionalism".[93]

"We have a Pope"

This traditional shout from the gathered crowds after the election of a new Pope motivates me to ask the question as to what exactly is the purpose of the office of a 'supreme' pastor, particularly in this context of the future of the Church? Is it one of government or of leadership, of 'chief constable' of the Catholic Church or of serving the communion of all Christians? Perhaps there is a need to first answer the question as to whether it was Jesus' intention that one man (or woman) should possess 'the keys to the kingdom of heaven', i.e. the authoritative truths of his 'good news' (gospel), or whether such a duty of preaching those truths was given to all his apostles? The two relevant passages in Matthew 16 and 18 on their own do not really help to decide one way or the other as the answer could be affirmative for both. However, it can be clearly seen throughout Jesus' ministry and in the writings of the New Testament that for his mission to the world to continue after his return to the Father in heaven, there needs to be leaders and guides who respond to the work of his Spirit. The first such persons were those apostles who as 'messengers' and 'witnesses' were chosen by Jesus. Nothing was laid down as to who their followers would be to bring the message and witness, the 'keys' to the kingdom of God, to those not yet born.

Common sense tells us that the first apostles were to pass on those truths to others who could continue to preserve and teach them and in turn pass them on to future generations. This

---

93   Rahner, p.30.

is what is meant by 'apostolic authority' being handed down through the generations, not the authority of a centurion or chief of police, nor that of a monarch, but the constant teaching of those chosen to pass on the central truths of the Gospel, the 'keys' to the reign of God in our hearts and minds. This is where their authority ends, for that is its fullness and purpose. Any extension of this to include 'government' of the people of God by the iron fist of an authoritarian regime is anti-Gospel and therefore anti-Christ.

If the above is true, what is the purpose of the office of pope as 'supreme pastor' in this gift of the 'keys'? Is it that which is set out in official doctrine in Canon Law as having *"supreme, full, immediate and universal power in the Church"*?[94] It is a fact of life, of the fact that humanity is not perfect yet, that among those chosen by men to keep and pass on the Gospel of Jesus Christ there will be some who fail to preserve and teach those Gospel truths. How can this 'authority' be protected from its abuse? How can its extension to government in the Church be excised and servant-ministry replace authoritarian control? Is this the role of the office of the pope, or is it the duty of the bishops who originally were the 'overseers' (Gk.episcopi) of the Church?

The problem with having a 'supremo' at the head of the Church is that this inevitably runs the risk of that person being a bad choice for the good of the Church, as history has shown. The presence of the Holy Spirit is not to take away human freedom for good or bad but to inspire and motivate those chosen to be leaders and guides. In the case of a Pope at the head of the Church, that freedom means that he is not immune from error or from abuse of his position, as history has shown. The necessary checks and balances have to come from within the Church, especially where such an office carries

---

94   1983 Code of Canon Law, canon 331.

with it the official teaching that on matters of faith and morals the office-holder's teachings are infallible when speaking *ex cathedra* i.e. from the 'chair' of St Peter. In the past, the bishops have attempted to remove a bad pope under their authority as apostolic successors, especially during the height of the Conciliar controversy of the 15th century, but the subsequent consolidation of the supreme office of 'pope'[95] has not prevented the controversy coming to the surface when there is some crisis involving the subject of authority in the Church.

I am not attempting to enter fully into this controversy over who should govern the Church, the body of bishops or the pope. For me, the issue, as is plain from what I have said above, is based on the notion of 'government', not on *who* should govern. If the office to govern is not part of Jesus' commission to the apostles, whether with Peter as head or not, then the argument about who has the final say in that duty of *governing* the Church is irrelevant. However, in matters of teaching, guiding and leading, there has to be those to whom the members of the Church can refer to in such matters of faith and morals, and as such there has to be a final arbiter where there is disagreement. This is where the notion of a 'hierarchy' has become the normal term to describe the different levels of competence. If such hierarchy only relates to matters of faith and morals then the question is one simply of what body or which person has the final teaching on a particular matter. However, if this notion of hierarchy extends further than guidance and takes on the character and practice of control in all aspects of the life of the individual believer through a systems of laws and sanctions, then it has gone outside of Jesus' commission and also antithetic to his Gospel.

---

95   cf. First Vatican Council, 1870.

Co-responsibility for the Church

What would be a better way of ensuring good servant-leadership which not only puts into practice the principal teachings of the Gospel but also reflects that communion, that Spirit-filled fellowship (koinonia) of the Church as the 'body of Christ'? I certainly do not have all the answers to this, but one way of facilitating expression of that fellowship can be seen in the idea and practice of 'synodality' to which I have referred in the chapter on authority. This is where those 'checks and balances' can be put into place in order to identify and remove those excesses of power and control. Such synodal structures, where representatives of the people of God are elected by their communities to reach consensus on forming policies in the administration of the Gospel within the body of the Church and electing those leaders and guides for the implementation of those policies, are a better way of ensuring that love and justice prevail. Even Benedict XVI, who in his later years as Pope resisted the changes that were needed, spoke of the need for lay people to be no longer viewed as "collaborators" of the clergy but "truly recognised as co-responsible for the Church's being and action."[96]

Those elected leaders and guides can be called 'bishops' or 'popes' or any other names to indicate their role but they cannot operate other than from within the 'sense of the faithful' (sensus fidelium) which is the work of the Holy Spirit of Christ. If they are elected representatives of the people they have been given a mandate, not only by their people but through them by Christ, to use their 'sense of the faith' (sensus fidei) to serve the Gospel. In this way the sense of the faithful becomes the check and balance on any movement towards authoritarianism and

---

96 "Ecclesial Convention of the Diocese of Rome" in "Osservatore Romano" 26th May 2009.

its many consequences detrimental to Christ's mission to the world.

How would this work out in practice? For example, the bishops as elected representatives of their communities could elect one or two of their own per country to represent a universal (catholic) body, similar to the present 'Synod of bishops' but who represent their communities and not, as at present, who possess a high degree of autonomy and who tend to ignore, with notable exceptions, the sense of the faithful. This is not to say that such bishops are simply to be spokespersons of the people. Rather, they have been given the trust of the people to use their talents and skills, their Christian wisdom and courage, to be their leaders and guides. However, because they are servants of Christ through his people who have chosen them, they can be removed from that role if they betray that trust. This would mean that the office of bishop as leader and guide is subject to the 'local Church' in the form of a synodal gathering in which representatives of the parishes are able to express their 'sense of the faith' and form a consensus on policies and actions for the common good. Any recommendation which would have national implications would then be passed to a regional synodal body for decision. In this way, there is less chance of the growth of authoritarianism, and would remove the present monarchical system of control which is always by its very nature liable to be authoritarian, even tyrannical, without such checks and balances. This does not mean that everything in the garden would be rosy! There will always be mistakes made as to choices of policy and personnel, but the checks and balances of a synodal system mean that the much more serious errors of authoritarianism and legalism which oppress the people of God are unable to flourish.

The history of the Church shows that at times certain leaders did in fact become tyrants when they became corrupted by their absolute power over the lives of members of the Church, and in some cases over the whole world.[97] The tyrannical practices of the Inquisition stemmed from this idea of absolute earthly and spiritual power being invested in the office of the Pope, who could express this through his bishops and priests, the effects of which were not only in this life but even after death. Even though recent Popes have not claimed such power, Catholics are still experiencing traces of that terrible time when anyone preaching and teaching against such power was treated as a 'heretic', being tortured for a confession and brutally put to death. Thank God that such ideas of punishing anyone who rejects such power of church officials is no longer accepted, but there are elements of that mind-set which still exist. For example, when Pope John Paul II declared that there can be no further discussion on the subject of women priests, it showed there still was in his mind the authority to control what members of the Church could say about the Christian faith. The furore created by such an attempt of what amounts to a form of mind-control, showed that such a view of the role of leadership in the Church is simply not acceptable by many of its members. Leaders and guides in the Church are not there to control but to draw people to Christ.

Local competence in the practice of synodality

The principle that all decisions in the Church should, if possible, be taken at the lowest level, i.e. at the local, not inferior, level, must be at the heart of the future administration if a synodal Church is to become a reality. The term used, 'subsidiarity', was very much in vogue in the years after Vatican II by those

---

97 Two examples among many: Pope Gregory VII (Hildebrand) 1073-85, who not only declared Popes above everything on earth but could also dethrone emperors and kings; Pope Innocent III in 1208 issued a call to arms against heretics which resulted in the massacre of the Cathars in France.

wishing to see a more decentralised Church administration. In the years following Vatican II the prophetic voice of the influential theologian Karl Rahner S.J. took this vision one step further with his challenging statement *"The Church of the future will be one built from below by basic communities as a result of free initiative and association."*[98] However, owing to the reactionary forces within the centralised organs of the administration, such a principle for the movement towards a less authoritarian approach, whereby the functions of a local community can be best fulfilled by itself, was never actualised.

Of what are these individual office-holders frightened? The fact is that if you, as a church office-holder, believe that as a leader of the people of God you were given the commission by Christ to *govern* his people, and that authority to govern necessarily means one of control, then the last thing you want is to surrender this to any kind of synodal structure at local level. But, if the people of God believe that Christ commissioned you to be a leader and guide as per the Gospel, and not a governor and controller of their lives, your leadership and guidance would be very much part of their decision-making for freedom to 'worship in spirit and truth'. At the end of the day, it is the right and responsibility of all Christians to make their own decision as to how they put that into practice, provided that decision is informed by that union of guidance from leaders with their own 'sense of the faith'. You cannot have real community, real fellowship, where there is no space for genuine dialogue in seeking consensus.

---

98 "The Shape of the Church to Come" 1972, p.108.

Pressure building up?

The problem is that in the present hierarchical system, which is in effect monarchical, there can never be genuine freedom for each of us to worship God in spirit and truth. For the principles of synodality (journeying together) and subsidiarity (local competence) to be put into practice, the present system of Church administration needs to be reformed if the danger of schism is to be avoided. This might seem to some as being a little dramatic, but there is increasing evidence in the world that populist pressures are producing schisms in the political sphere, where people are feeling disempowered by global forces beyond their control.[99] These movements are a sign of frustration with governments who continue to show scant regard to the values which the people identify as important for them.[100] Much of this frustration arises from their experience of successive administrations paying lip-service to their perceived social justice principles.

The church communities, particularly of the Roman Catholic Church, are not immune from these trends, because the underlying frustrations with centralised 'authorities' can be the same. For example, in the Roman Catholic Church, the rise of many movements working for reform of the structures, policies and practices of administration so that there is genuine communion, genuine meeting of mind and hearts, is indicative of the Spirit-inspired 'sense of the faithful' becoming more courageous in its expression.[101] The danger is that if the present Church authorities do not heed such frustration and therefore

---

99 George Osborne & Michael Bloomberg in art. In "The Times" newspaper 27.2.2017.
100 The "Brexit" vote in the UK in 2016 is one of the signs, as are those "far-right" movements in USA and Europe.
101 E.g. "A Call To Action" (ACTA) UK; "We Are Church" UK & Europe; "American Catholic Council" USA.

look to themselves in identifying the fault-lines, many of the so-called 'faithful' will go their own way and seek expression in Christian communities owing no allegiance to an institution which has moved a good distance away from the teachings of the Gospel of Jesus Christ. Although such schisms are by their very nature at variance with the Christian principles of 'the common way' (synodality), the history of the Church shows that very often it needed a crisis for its leaders to be forced into realising they had strayed far from 'the way' of Jesus Christ. Unfortunately, there were two momentous schisms, the 11th century break between the churches of Constantinople and Rome with each claiming the true apostolic authority, and the 16th century Reformation where the Popes and hierarchy failed to recognise and address the mostly legitimate complaints of the Reformers. Both have gone their own way, with further breaks among themselves as time went on.

In all crises such as these schisms there takes place a certain re-focusing on those issues which are at the centre of the storms. This can either be good for the Christian church or can lead to an even greater movement away from the 'way' of Jesus Christ as taught by him and his first apostles. In the case of the Roman wing of the catholic Church, the view that all authority and power is invested in the office of Pope became even more entrenched, so much so that this 'mystique' of such power led to the complete identification of God's will with the institutional form of authority.[102] Despite all the changes which have occurred since then, this mind-set and its expression through the office of Pope and bishops/priests, is still the most serious obstacle to a genuine 'reformation' of ideas and practices. If the New Testament reference in Matthew's gospel of Jesus appointing Peter as the 'rock' of the future Church

---

102 Yves Congar O.P. "Power and Poverty in the Church" 1964. p.71.

is understood[103] as denoting the subsequent development of the position of a supreme leader as 'pope' or 'pontiff' (bridge builder) as we know it today, then that position can only be one of serving, not governing, the unity of faith, hope and love which is the purpose of the Church.

I am sure there are many Catholics who would say that surely all these popes, bishops and priests cannot have been wrong in continuing their understanding of their roles, their authority, and above all of the truths of the Gospel. However, the underlying fault is not in their individual personal dedication to their given roles. There is much evidence of witness to Christ and love for those in their care in their everyday activities. No, the fault-line is in their allegiance to certain teachings about what the nature and form should be for administering leadership in the Church. These teachings are fundamental to their understanding of their position and role, and are at the core of their training and regularly confirmed by subsequent instructions. Even at Vatican II, the bishops could not shake off such ingrained ideas.

The fact that there are a large number, world-wide, of men in positions of bishop, deacon and priest, is not in itself an indication that there is biblical and theological justification for the forms and practices of those offices. In the history of mankind, there have been many occasions where large numbers of individuals, whether in groups or not, have been led astray by following a particular path. For example, the Israelites themselves were often being pulled back by God's prophets from adopting ideas and practices which would lead them away from his Law. Numbers are no indication of possession of truth, and in fact the sheer weight of numbers, together with their

---

103 It is significant that the similar reference in Mark's gospel, which precedes Matthew, at 8:27-30, does not mention such an appointment. Luke also does not mention it in his similar reference, and John makes no reference to that occasion.

appearance of having authority, can obscure the very truths of their cause. Jesus himself was a radical who resisted authorities, to the point of death, when they attempted to use their weight against him.

If the Church is to be 'fit for purpose', its leaders and pastors must relinquish all claims to govern and control the faith of the people of God so that they are really free to worship 'in spirit and truth', and therefore reflect the true image of God to those around them. Only in this way can we be truly "honest to God."

****

Lightning Source UK Ltd.
Milton Keynes UK
UKHW04f0841260918
329500UK00001B/17/P